MACAT

T0273452

An Analysis of

Paul Kennedy's

The Rise and Fall of the Great Powers

Riley Quinn

ROUTLEDGE

Published by Macat International Ltd
24:13 Coda Centre, 189 Munster Road, London SW6 6AW.

Distributed exclusively by Routledge
2 Park Square, Milton Park, Abingdon, Oxon OX14 4RN
711 Third Avenue, New York, NY 10017, USA

Routledge is an imprint of the Taylor & Francis Group, an informa business

Copyright © 2017 by Macat International Ltd
Macat International has asserted its right under the Copyright, Designs and Patents Act
1988 to be identified as the copyright holder of this work.

www.macat.com
info@macat.com

Cataloguing in Publication Data
A catalogue record for this book is available from the British Library.
Library of Congress Cataloguing-in-Publication Data is available upon request.
Cover illustration: Kim Thompson
ISBN 978-1-912302-68-0 (hardback)
ISBN 978-1-912128-15-0 (paperback)
ISBN 978-1-912281-56-5 (e-book)

Notice
The information in this book is designed to orientate readers of the work under analysis,
to elucidate and contextualise its key ideas and themes, and to aid in the development
of critical thinking skills. It is not meant to be used, nor should it be used, as a
substitute for original thinking or in place of original writing or research. References and
notes are provided for informational purposes and their presence does not constitute
endorsement of the information or opinions therein. This book is presented solely for
educational purposes. It is sold on the understanding that the publisher is not engaged
to provide any scholarly advice. The publisher has made every effort to ensure that
this book is accurate and up-to-date, but makes no warranties or representations with
regard to the completeness or reliability of the information it contains. The information
and the opinions provided herein are not guaranteed or warranted to produce particular
results and may not be suitable for students of every ability. The publisher shall not be
liable for any loss, damage or disruption arising from any errors or omissions, or from
the use of this book, including, but not limited to, special, incidental, consequential or
other damages caused, or alleged to have been caused, directly or indirectly, by the
information contained within.

CONTENTS

WAYS IN TO THE TEXT

Who Is Paul Kennedy?   9

What Does *The Rise and Fall of the Great Powers* Say?   10

Why Does *The Rise and Fall of the Great Powers* Matter?   11

SECTION 1: INFLUENCES

Module 1: The Author and the Historical Context   14

Module 2: Academic Context   19

Module 3: The Problem   24

Module 4: The Author's Contribution   29

SECTION 2: IDEAS

Module 5: Main Ideas   35

Module 6: Secondary Ideas   40

Module 7: Achievement   46

Module 8: Place in the Author's Work   51

SECTION 3: IMPACT

Module 9: The First Responses   56

Module 10: The Evolving Debate   61

Module 11: Impact and Influence Today   66

Module 12: Where Next?   71

Glossary of Terms   76

People Mentioned in the Text   86

Works Cited   94

THE MACAT LIBRARY

The Macat Library is a series of unique academic explorations of seminal works in the humanities and social sciences – books and papers that have had a significant and widely recognised impact on their disciplines. It has been created to serve as much more than just a summary of what lies between the covers of a great book. It illuminates and explores the influences on, ideas of, and impact of that book. Our goal is to offer a learning resource that encourages critical thinking and fosters a better, deeper understanding of important ideas.

Each publication is divided into three Sections: Influences, Ideas, and Impact. Each Section has four Modules. These explore every important facet of the work, and the responses to it.

This Section-Module structure makes a Macat Library book easy to use, but it has another important feature. Because each Macat book is written to the same format, it is possible (and encouraged!) to cross-reference multiple Macat books along the same lines of inquiry or research. This allows the reader to open up interesting interdisciplinary pathways.

To further aid your reading, lists of glossary terms and people mentioned are included at the end of this book (these are indicated by an asterisk [*] throughout) – as well as a list of works cited.

Macat has worked with the University of Cambridge to identify the elements of critical thinking and understand the ways in which six different skills combine to enable effective thinking.
Three allow us to fully understand a problem; three more give us the tools to solve it. Together, these six skills make up the **PACIER** model of critical thinking. They are:

ANALYSIS – understanding how an argument is built
EVALUATION – exploring the strengths and weaknesses of an argument
INTERPRETATION – understanding issues of meaning

CREATIVE THINKING – coming up with new ideas and fresh connections
PROBLEM-SOLVING – producing strong solutions
REASONING – creating strong arguments

To find out more, visit **WWW.MACAT.COM.**

CRITICAL THINKING AND *THE RISE AND FALL OF THE GREAT POWERS*

Primary critical thinking skill: PROBLEM-SOLVING
Secondary critical thinking skill: EVALUATION

Paul Kennedy owes a great deal to the editor who persuaded him to add a final chapter to this study of the factors that contributed to the rise and fall of European powers since the age of Spain's Philip II. This tailpiece indulged in what was, for an historian, a most unusual activity: it looked into the future. Pondering whether the United States would ultimately suffer the same decline as every imperium that preceded it, it was this chapter that made *The Rise and Fall of the Great Powers* a dinner party talking point in Washington government circles. In so doing, it elevated Kennedy to the ranks of public intellectuals whose opinions were canvassed on matters of state policy.

From a strictly academic point of view, the virtues of Kennedy's work lie elsewhere, and specifically in his flair for asking the sort of productive questions that characterize a great problem-solver. Kennedy's work is an example of an increasingly rare genre – a work of comparative history that transcends the narrow confines of state– and era–specific studies to identify the common factors that underpin the successes and failures of highly disparate states.

Kennedy's prime contribution is the now-famous concept of 'imperial overstretch,' the idea that empires fall largely because the military commitments they acquire during the period of their rise ultimately become too much to sustain once they lose the economic competitive edge that had projected them to dominance in the first place. Earlier historians may have glimpsed this central truth, and even applied it in studies of specific polities, but it took a problem-solver of Kennedy's ability to extend the analysis convincingly across half a millennium.

ABOUT THE AUTHOR OF THE ORIGINAL WORK

Born in the north of England in 1945, towards the end of World War II, historian **Paul Kennedy** was the first person in his working-class family to attend university. He earned a degree at Newcastle University and went on to gain a Ph.D. from Oxford. Watching the British Empire shrink as he grew up, Kennedy developed a lifelong interest in the factors that cause great powers to wither. He has spent the majority of his career teaching in the United States, where he chaired the international history department at Yale. Kennedy has become a respected commentator and writer on global affairs, as well as advising both the United Nations and the United States. He was made a Commander of the Order of the British Empire in 2001.

ABOUT THE AUTHOR OF THE ANALYSIS

Riley Quinn holds master's degrees in politics and international relations from both LSE and the University of Oxford.

ABOUT MACAT

GREAT WORKS FOR CRITICAL THINKING

Macat is focused on making the ideas of the world's great thinkers accessible and comprehensible to everybody, everywhere, in ways that promote the development of enhanced critical thinking skills.

It works with leading academics from the world's top universities to produce new analyses that focus on the ideas and the impact of the most influential works ever written across a wide variety of academic disciplines. Each of the works that sit at the heart of its growing library is an enduring example of great thinking. But by setting them in context – and looking at the influences that shaped their authors, as well as the responses they provoked – Macat encourages readers to look at these classics and game-changers with fresh eyes. Readers learn to think, engage and challenge their ideas, rather than simply accepting them.

'Macat offers an amazing first-of-its-kind tool for
interdisciplinary learning and research. Its focus on works
that transformed their disciplines and its rigorous approach,
drawing on the world's leading experts and educational institutions,
opens up a world-class education to anyone.'
Andreas Schleicher,
Director for Education and Skills, Organisation for Economic
Co-operation and Development

'Macat is taking on some of the major challenges in university
education ... They have drawn together a strong team of active
academics who are producing teaching materials that are
novel in the breadth of their approach.'
Prof Lord Broers,
former Vice-Chancellor of the University of Cambridge

'The Macat vision is exceptionally exciting. It focuses
upon new modes of learning which analyse and explain seminal texts
which have profoundly influenced world thinking and so social and
economic development. It promotes the kind of critical thinking
which is essential for any society and economy.
This is the learning of the future.'
Rt Hon Charles Clarke, former UK Secretary of State for Education

'The Macat analyses provide immediate access to the critical
conversation surrounding the books that have shaped their
respective discipline, which will make them an invaluable resource
to all of those, students and teachers, working in the field.'
Professor William Tronzo, University of California at San Diego

WAYS IN TO THE TEXT

KEY POINTS

- The English historian Paul Kennedy, born in 1945, spent most of his career in the United States and achieved prominence toward the end of the Cold War* (a period of tension between the US and the communist Soviet Union* that began following World War II and ended with the collapse of European communism in 1991).

- According to *The Rise and Fall of the Great Powers* (1987), powerful nations owe their dominance more to their economic strength than their military strength.

- The work made a very important argument that the United States may be vulnerable to decline in the future; the book's conclusions, however, continue to be debated.

Who Is Paul Kennedy?

The English historian Paul Kennedy, author of *The Rise and Fall of the Great Powers* (1987), was born in 1945 to a working-class family in the north of England. The first of his family to attend university, he graduated in history with first-class honors from Newcastle University.* He completed his doctorate at the University of Oxford* before moving to the United States to become chair in international history at Yale University.*

Rise and Fall, a book dealing with the politics of power at a time of great instability, was timely. It was published in 1987, just a few years before the end of the Cold War and the shift in the international balance of power that followed. During the Cold War, a period of heightened global tension, the United States and the Soviet Union (the USSR) engaged in covert operations, nuclear posturing, and proxy wars against one another, although the hostility never broke into open conflict. In the late 1980s, America had taken on a newly aggressive posture, and the Soviet Union stretched its budget to match the threat.

The book earned Kennedy a sort of academic and literary celebrity and saw him became a prolific commentator on global affairs. His scholarly work focused on the importance of international institutions (such as the United Nations).* His writing on great power politics found a home both in the general interest press and in journals aimed at foreign policy professionals such as *Foreign Affairs*.*

What Does *The Rise and Fall of the Great Powers* Say?

In *Rise and Fall*, Kennedy argues that shifts in power around the globe follow a consistent pattern. Beginning with Europe in 1500, Kennedy looks at two dimensions of the predominant European power at the time, the Habsburg dynasty.* Members of this prosperous family of Austrian Spanish descent had managed to claim a range of powerful positions across Europe. Kennedy concludes that the Habsburgs lost power because their military commitments outpaced their economic prosperity. That is to say, they fought too many wars for their treasury to handle—a situation we might today call "imperial overreach." Diminished economic strength reduced their military strength, which in turn created more economic weakness.

So Kennedy sees factors like military strategy and the economy reinforcing the rise and the fall of great powers. He applies the same paradigm* (conceptual model) to the great powers in the centuries that followed: Spain, France, Britain, Germany, and the United States. Kennedy is not an "economic determinist." That is, he does not think underlying economic conditions predetermine the events of history. Instead, he believes the economic resources at their disposal give statesmen more or fewer options. Over time, more prosperous states— those with more options—remain more likely to prevail.

What made *Rise and Fall* such an important work was not its analysis of the sixteenth century. The work's later, predictive chapters applied those historical lessons to the great powers of the twentieth century. Kennedy predicted that the United States risked falling into the same pattern that had afflicted older empires. With its military commitments growing beyond its capacity to pay, America risked decline. During the 1990s, when the United States' leadership of the world appeared unchallenged, this assumption was not popular.

At the opening of the twenty-first century, the cracks in US predominance began to show. The terrorist attacks of September 11, 2001 ("9/11")* provoked the US into prolonged military occupations in the developing world; meanwhile, China began to claim an increasing share of world productivity. Following the global financial crisis of 2007–8, scholars began to reexamine Kennedy's question: was the United States in decline? American foreign policy entered an introspective phase. Should it increase its commitments abroad to combat rising powers? Should it decrease its commitments abroad to conserve a diminishing resource base?

The debate is far from over, and as it rages the world has only become more unstable and troubled.

Why Does *The Rise and Fall of the Great Powers* Matter?

While *Rise and Fall* offers a detailed survey of the events that have defined world history for the last 500 years, Kennedy sees history as more than a list of events. He seeks to *explain* events. What patterns can we uncover in historical events? What can we say about their causes?

Rise and Fall helps readers understand *why* the events happened. The book serves as a key introduction to studies in both history and political science.

The work also offers readers a keen perspective on current affairs. Policymakers and pundits have long debated the question of whether or not the United States is facing decline. *Rise and Fall* suggests that the answer might be that it is. But it also argues that "declinism"*—the belief that one's nation is in irreversible decline—might be an oversimplification. Is it really just a matter of economics? Does "identity" matter? Is the role of global leader worth the struggle required?

Understanding how these two strands of thinking—large-scale historical analysis and the current-affairs perspective of "declinism"— compete requires critical thinking. Moreover, *Rise and Fall* helps readers understand the factors that make one school of thought more popular than another. Do the foundations of "declinism" hold up? The classic case of "imperial overreach" involves administering foreign territories where a country has security concerns. American foreign policy, both during and since the Cold War, has been a cause of concern for some thinkers (including Kennedy), who believe that the country's foreign adventures are imprudent.

Today, many voices argue that the US should follow some course or other in response to the actions of Syria, China, Russia, and so on. *Rise and Fall* introduces readers to the long-term consequences of the range of decisions: Intervene and risk overstretch; do not intervene and risk irrelevance. The work offers us a way to examine assertions that may include wild or unsupported assumptions.

SECTION 1
INFLUENCES

MODULE 1
THE AUTHOR AND THE
HISTORICAL CONTEXT

KEY POINTS

- *Rise and Fall* argues that a state's military predominance must be underpinned by prosperity relative to other states.

- Kennedy's study of history fostered a keen interest in the great empires (or more recently the international institutions) that govern the world.

- *Rise and Fall* appeared toward the end of the long period of global tension known as the Cold War,* when the United States stepped up its military commitments abroad under the "Reagan doctrine"*—an increase in military spending designed to pressure the Soviet Union.*

Why Read this Text?

Paul Kennedy's *The Rise and Fall of the Great Powers* is an epic exploration of history. His timeframe stretches from European dynastic* power struggles—struggles between aristocratic families for the right to rule—at the birth of the modern nation-state in 1500, up to the tail end of the Cold War.* The book was published in 1987; the Cold War ended with the collapse of the communist Soviet Union four years later. Rather than offering an account of history as a sequence of consecutive events, he explains how the underlying economic power of competing states produced grand battles and diplomatic intrigue.

States succeed *in relation to their competitors* when they preserve the most vibrant economy, pursue technological development, and avoid diverting too many resources to the military. "Imperial overreach" however, may cause successful states to falter: their confidence grows

> **66** [The United States will] contain and over time
> reverse Soviet expansionism by competing effectively
> on a sustained basis with the Soviet Union in all
> international arenas—particularly in the overall military
> balance and in geographical regions of priority concern
> to the United States. **99**
>
> United States *National Security Decision Directive 75*, 1983

as their strategic commitments grow, and with that, the size of their military; eventually the economy can no longer support the strategic commitments made by the political state, and the "Great Power" shrinks.

This book applies the same analytical method to all its subjects, whether Imperial Spain* between the fifteenth and the nineteenth centuries, the British Empire,* or the modern United States.

Author's Life

Paul Kennedy was born in the northern English city of Newcastle to a working-class family in 1945. In an interview with the English newspaper the *Guardian*,* he said the family assumed that he would start working when he left school.[1] He surprised everyone, however, first when he went on to study history at Newcastle University,* and then when he sought an advanced degree, a DPhil at St. Antony's College* (an all-graduate college with a large American population) at Oxford University.* At Oxford, he worked under British military historian and strategist Sir Basil Liddell Hart.*

Growing up at the very end of the British Empire inspired Kennedy to write about "great powers," and specifically to focus on what happens to those that engage in imperial overreach: Kennedy wondered if he might enter the imperial service, but "by the time I reached college [in 1963], almost all of that distant empire had become independent."[2] Finding it so unusual that a small island off the coast of Europe might govern a quarter of the world, he decided to study the phenomenon of the "great power."[3] In 1982, the United Kingdom and Argentina clashed over the Falkland Islands, small islands in the South Atlantic with a combined population of only a few thousand. Although the British won the Falklands War,* the conflict highlighted the extent to which the British have retreated from their overseas possessions.

Kennedy's academic career swiftly took him to Yale University* in the United States. While there, he published *Rise and Fall*—and the book catapulted him to academic superstardom. Soon he had been tapped as an advisor to both the United Nations* and the United States government. His work with the United Nations led him to write *The Parliament of Man*, a study of the role, shortcomings, and potential of the UN.[4] From empire to global governance, Kennedy writes about what he sees as the most important issues facing the world today.

Author's Background

A period of tension between the capitalist* United States and the communist* Soviet Union, the Cold War had defined international politics for nearly five decades beginning with the close of World War II.* (Capitalism is the economic and social system dominant in the Western world, in which industry is held in private hands; communism is a political ideology according to which property is held in common hands and the means of production—the tools and resources required for production—are administered by the state.)

While the Cold War did not involve direct conflict, it did produce proxy wars, such as the Korean War* (1950–3) and the Vietnam War* (1955–75), in which the United States fought the Soviet Union and China indirectly, and some terrifying near-wars such as the Cuban Missile Crisis* of 1962—an event that very nearly led to all-out nuclear conflict over the stationing of Soviet missiles in Cuba. In short, the Soviets and the Americans saw each other as existential threats. The possibility of nuclear destruction loomed large over the entire world.

Kennedy had originally planned to release *Rise and Fall* in 1986. If he had, the book would have dealt with great power dynamics only up to the end of World War II.*[5] But, having "started looking at the unbalanced fiscal policies and heavy military spending of the US and the USSR" in the late 1980s, he realized he needed to add these current events to the book and postponed its release for a year.[6]

The imbalances Kennedy mentioned stem in many ways from the "Reagan doctrine," named for US president Ronald Reagan* and implemented with the aim of increasing pressure on the Soviet Union. An ideological hardliner, Reagan dubbed the Soviet Union the "evil empire" and called for a massive American arms build-up. He also channeled significantly increased support (in the form of arms, money, and training) to anti-Soviet groups plotting the overthrow of their communist-aligned governments around the world.[7]

By spending just a fraction more of its income on these strategic goals, the US intensified the pressure on an already strained Soviet domestic economy.[8] Soviet spending on its military, matching US commitments, consumed up to one-quarter of its total national income; it seemed unlikely that this state of affairs could be maintained.[9] In this period, with an internationally committed United States and a wobbling Soviet Union, Kennedy wrote his history of great power politics.

In certain ways, the historical patterns he had identified as far back as the 1500s still held true at the time he published the book. He had expected instability and violence to accompany the fall of any great power, but when the economically and militarily overcommitted government of the USSR fell, just four years after he published this book, the Cold War came to an unexpectedly quick and peaceful end by 1991. This outcome would have taken Kennedy by surprise, because he believed the fall of great powers was accompanied by military conflict, where the weakened great power would be defeated by the rising great power.

NOTES

1   John Crace, "Paul Kennedy: Neocons' Worst Nightmare," *Guardian*, February 5, 2008, accessed September 3, 2015, http://www.theguardian.com/education/2008/feb/05/academicexperts.highereducationprofile.

2   Paul Kennedy, "The Imperial Mind: A Historian's Education in the Ways of Empire," *The Atlantic*, January 2008, accessed September 3, 2015, http://www.theatlantic.com/magazine/archive/2008/01/the-imperial-mind/306566/.

3   Kennedy, "The Imperial Mind."

4   Huw Richards, "Redrawing the Big Picture," *Times Higher Education*, August 28, 2008, accessed September 2, 2015, https://www.timeshighereducation.co.uk/features/redrawing-the-big-picture/403290.article.

5   Crace, "Paul Kennedy."

6   Crace, "Paul Kennedy."

7   Raymond L. Garthoff, *The Great Transition: American–Soviet Relations and the End of the Cold War* (Washington, DC: Brookings Institution, 1994), 8–9.

8   Garthoff, *The Great Transition*, 78.

9   Walter LaFeber, *America, Russia, and the Cold War, 1945–2002* (New York: McGraw Hill, 2002), 335.

MODULE 2
ACADEMIC CONTEXT

KEY POINTS

- International history explains the present day at the international level through an analysis of the patterns of past events.

- While classical diplomatic history concerned itself with great men and large events, modern approaches to history examine underlying patterns; large events require explanation, and are not considered causes in themselves.

- Kennedy's focus on the economic foundations on which relationships between great powers are built reflects the work of his supervisors at Oxford, the British historians A. J. P. Taylor* and John Gallagher.*

The Work In Its Context

Paul Kennedy's *The Rise and Fall of the Great Powers* (1987) falls into the category of international history. Traditionally history has focused on "great men" and diplomatic relations between states—things to be explained. Modern approaches like Kennedy's focus on the underlying patterns of history—things doing the explaining. The eighteenth-century German historian Friedrich Schiller* articulated the discipline's statement of purpose in 1789. The international historian must "select from the stream of events those that exercise an essential, unmistakable, and easily comprehensible influence on the *present* shape of the world and the situation of the contemporary generation."[1]

We must also examine *Rise and Fall* in the context of the field of international relations.* Formerly a subset of historical studies, international relations became its own discipline in 1920 with the foundation of the first dedicated department at Aberystwyth

> ❝ In retrospect, though many were guilty, none was innocent. The purpose of political activity is to provide peace and prosperity; and in this every statesman failed, for whatever reason. This is a story without heroes, and perhaps even without villains. ❞
>
> A. J. P. Taylor, *The Origins of the Second World War*

University* in Wales. Rather than seeking to explain patterns in past events, the discipline "seeks to explain why international events occur the way they do."[2] So while international relations tends to be more interested in making a general theory of state action, the discipline of international history tends to focus more on explaining trends that extend beyond state borders. In practice, however, the division remains imperfect and they have more commonalities than differences.

Overview of the Field

The practice of diplomacy became increasingly "professionalized" in Europe in the 1800s. At the same time, history became increasingly focused on explaining foreign policies and grand power politics.[3] Nineteenth-century German scholar Leopold von Ranke* was likely the first modern diplomatic historian. His concept of *Primat der Außenpolitik** (meaning, roughly, "the primacy of foreign policy") explained the history of Europe through external relationships between states. As he saw it, states "organize all [their] internal re-sources for the purpose of self-preservation" against threats posed by other states.[4] His work, including his famous *History of the Latin and Teutonic Peoples* (1824),[5] addresses the long-term roots of conflicts between entire societies as managed by great personalities. But perhaps the most important aspect of Ranke's work is that he relies on "real data" (especially diplomatic archives) to present the narrative of events as they truly happened.

Ranke's approach persisted until the middle of the twentieth century, when scholars began shift their focus. Instead of narrating history through the dramatic decisions and relationships of great men, they examined the underlying forces and the actions of common men. The influential French historian Fernand Braudel's* 1949 book, *The Mediterranean and the Mediterranean World in the Age of Philip II,* * illustrates this shift to "social" history.

Braudel examined Europe in the sixteenth century not through the thought-out diplomacy between "great men" (kings and generals), but by looking at the *longue durée**—the slow evolution of change. Braudel found these changes in geographic division, in the development of science and technology, and in economic matters. "Resounding events," Braudel wrote, "are often only momentary outbursts," and are only understandable in terms of "larger movements" underneath the surface.[6] Long-term history did not see diplomacy as explaining outcomes, but as one of the outcomes to be explained by sub-surface forces.

While the *Annales** school of history with which Fernand Braudel was notably associated focused on *longue durée** history (that is, on the effects economic developments have had on historical outcomes), the twentieth-century American scholar Immanuel Wallerstein's* world systems analysis* aimed to show how the economic and social system of capitalism* formed the roots of a single international system. "In the late fifteenth and early sixteenth century," Wallerstein wrote, "there came into existence what we may call a European World Economy" as capitalism began to take root and expand.[7] This world economy gives us a kind of global division of labor: "core" states in Europe and North America engage in high-value production, extracting cheap labor and raw materials from the "periphery" colonialized or otherwise overpowered states in the global South. "Capitalism," argued Wallerstein, "as an economic mode is based on the fact that the economic factors operate within an arena larger than that which any political entity can totally control," which makes possible "the constant economic expansion of the world system."[8]

Academic Influences

Historians A. J. P. Taylor and John Andrew Gallagher, Kennedy's supervisors at Oxford, both studied the long-term diplomatic history of Britain. Taylor's 1954 work, *The Struggle for Mastery in Europe 1848–1918*, examined the diplomatic and economic origins of World War I.* The introduction to *Struggle* makes comparisons between great powers through the analysis of hard data concerning things such as manpower, coal output, and steel production to assess their genuine strength.[9] "The statesmen of Europe," Taylor pointed out, "looked at political appearances more than economic realities."[10] But Taylor primarily based his assessment of nineteenth-century power politics on diplomatic maneuvering. For example, he believed that the ambitiousness of German leadership, rather than some underlying material factor, caused World War I.

Kennedy's other academic mentor at Oxford was John Gallagher, a historian whose academic fame stemmed from a 1961 book he coauthored exploring British imperialism in Africa. *Africa and the Victorians: The Official Mind of Imperialism* reads more like theory than history. As Gallagher wrote, "We have not tried to write a history of the regions of Africa during the nineteenth century;" instead, Africa was "the hook on which we hang hypotheses about nationalism and world politics."[11] Once again, economy played a crucial role: "From Europe stemmed the economic drive to integrate" foreign regions as "markets and investment." Security played a secondary role, as the great powers tried to preempt others from expanding by increasing their own territorial footprint.[12]

It should be noted that Gallagher and Wallerstein (who argued that all states operate according to an economic system larger than any particular nation) differ in certain important respects. Gallagher argued that individual states secured foreign territory to support their enterprises abroad; for Wallerstein, all states played their parts in a larger system.

NOTES

1   Friedrich Schiller, quoted in Gordon A. Craig, "The Historian and the Study of International Relations," *American Historical Review* 88, no. 1 (1983): 3.

2   Tobjorn Knutsen, *History of International Relations Theory* (Manchester: Manchester University Press, 1997), 6.

3   Patrick Finney, "Introduction: What is International History?" in *Palgrave Advances in International History*, ed. Patrick Finney (Basingstoke: Palgrave Macmillan, 2005), 1.

4   Theodore H. von Laue, *Leopold Ranke, The Formative Years* (Princeton, NJ: Princeton University Press, 1950), 167.

5   Leopold von Ranke, *History of the Latin and Teutonic Peoples 1494–1514*, trans. G. R. Dennis (London: George Bell and Sons, 1909).

6   Fernand Braudel, *The Mediterranean and Mediterranean World in the Age of Philip II*, trans. Siân Reynolds (New York: Harper & Row, 1972), 21.

7   Immanuel Wallerstein, *The Modern World System I: Capitalist Agriculture and the Origins of the European World-Economy in the Sixteenth Century, with a New Prologue* (Berkeley: University of California Press, 2011), 15.

8   Wallerstein, *The Modern World System*, 348.

9   A. J. P. Taylor, *The Struggle for Mastery in Europe 1848–1918* (Oxford: Oxford University Press, 1969), xxvi–xxxiv.

10 Taylor, *Struggle for Mastery*, xxxii.

11 Ronald Robinson et al., *Africa and the Victorians: The Official Mind of Imperialism* (Basingstoke: Macmillan, 1981), xxv.

12 Robinson et al., *Africa and the Victorians*, 485.

MODULE 3
THE PROBLEM

KEY POINTS

- Scholars were asking the question: when looking at the politics of the most powerful states, what forces explain the broad patterns of history?

- Two broad approaches dominated: scholars of international relations emphasized structural factors; scholars concerned with "great men" emphasized individual decisions.

- Looking at a longer arc of history than his contemporaries, Kennedy focused on both structural trends *and* individual responses.

Core Question

Paul Kennedy's *The Rise and Fall of the Great Powers* (1987) is relevant to a question that political theorists and historians had already been considering for many years when the book was published: what is the nature of the underlying forces driving political outcomes?

Explanations of political events and theories of statecraft developed according to the methods of *longue durée** ("long term") analysis (an approach taken by historians of the *Annales* school,* who were concerned with historical—often social—changes over the long term) had been being made for more than a century. Theorists looked to identify underlying forces in order to predict future outcomes; historians looked to identify the underlying forces to explain past events.

The perilous nuclear standoff between the United States and the Soviet Union* and their allies that defined the Cold War,* however,

> ❝ History, as anyone who has spent any time at all studying it would surely know, has a habit of making bad prophets out of both those who make and those who chronicle it. ❞
>
> John Lewis Gaddis, "The Long Peace"

made it more essential than ever to answer this important question. With both sides possessing nuclear weapons, predicting the outcome of this tense period seemed to be literally a matter of life and death. It was particularly urgent that scholars and politicians should come to understand the present through the lessons of the past—the purpose of the study of international relations since the discipline's inception.

Moreover, the great powers had become more interdependent by the end of World War II* than other great powers had been in the past. For Kennedy, the "large powers"—the United States, the USSR,* China, Japan, and the European community—were required to manage and exercise their economic and military power in such a way that they would not overexert it and sow the seeds of their own decline.[1]

The Participants

One of the other key perspectives on great power politics came from twentieth-century American political scientist Kenneth Waltz.* His *Theory of International Politics*, published in 1979, presented an entirely theory-driven (that is, non-historical) picture of global politics. Waltz believed the particular "goings on" of individual states remained entirely incidental to the course of history. After all, war has always been an outcome of relationships between great powers, regardless of how states are governed or by whom.[2] Waltz's theory was that, since the international sphere was anarchic* (that is, it was ungoverned), states must look after their own security. From this perspective, all states have the same interest (survival) and the same (military) means to ensure it.[3] We can only compare states on the basis of their power.

Waltz often compares states to billiard balls, which differ only in size and weight; for him, states differ only in their material capabilities. History, then, merely recounts the outcome of the balance of power. Following his theory into the present day of the 1970s, Waltz believed that the enemy states of the Soviet Union and the United States would never fight because the risk was too great. While both were powerful, neither was powerful enough to prevail. International relations scholars call this the stable condition of bipolarity.*

Kennedy's colleague at Yale, the American historian John Lewis Gaddis,* presented a different answer: for him, "if the structure of bipolarity in itself encouraged stability, so too did certain inherent characteristics of the bilateral Soviet–American relationship."[4] Just as the balance of power mattered, so did the players in this balance. Gaddis sought to explain why the relationship between the Soviet Union and the United States—though certainly not friendly— remained so stable. He believes that the superpowers* (politically, militarily, and economically dominant nations) could maintain peace so long as they followed certain patterns of behavior:

- respecting one another's spheres of influence* (the areas in which they wield special authority)
- avoiding military confrontation
- avoiding nuclear confrontation
- accepting injustice so long as it is predictable (that is, injustice that would not come as a surprise or provoke a response—for example, the existence of political prisoners was accepted)
- avoiding interference in one another's domestic politics.[5]

Gaddis explains the historical outcome of "stability" by examining the choices made by the superpowers rather than the nature of the superpowers themselves.

The Contemporary Debate

Kennedy's line of inquiry remained uniquely ambitious for his time. He never directly comments on either Waltz's or Gaddis's visions of history. Though, to make some broad generalizations, Kennedy differed from Waltz because he delved into the particular, and from Gaddis because he aimed for the generalizable: "Precisely because neither economic historians nor military historians had entered this field, the story [of the grand history of all great powers] had simply suffered from neglect."[6]

Essentially, Kennedy saw work in the fields of international relations and history—even studies sometimes described as "big" history, which offer explanations of all of human history with reference to some single factor—as suffering from a blind spot. They did not focus on the *longue durée* history of great powers as a phenomenon. Gaddis focused on a particular great power or group of great powers; Waltz focused on power in general. "What most readers and listeners wanted," Kennedy suggested, "was *more* detail, *more* coverage of the background, simply because there was no study available."[7]

Kennedy liked to paraphrase the nineteenth-century German statesman Otto von Bismarck:* "all of these Powers are traveling on 'the stream of Time,' which they can 'neither create nor direct,' but upon which they can 'steer with more or less skill and experience.'"[8] Kennedy's theory formed the middle way between the international relations theorist and the historian.

NOTES

1   Paul Kennedy, *The Rise and Fall of the Great Powers* (New York: Vintage Books, 1989), 540.

2   Kenneth Waltz, *Theory of International Politics* (Reading: Addison Wesley, 1979), 65.

3   Waltz, *Theory*, 99.

4   John Lewis Gaddis, "The Long Peace: Elements of Stability in the Postwar International System," *International Security* 10, no. 4 (1986): 110.

5   Gaddis, "The Long Peace," 133–8.

6   Kennedy, *Rise and Fall*, xxv.

7   Kennedy, *Rise and Fall*, xxv.

8   Kennedy, *Rise and Fall*, 540.

MODULE 4
THE AUTHOR'S CONTRIBUTION

KEY POINTS

- Kennedy aimed to present a history of powerful European states from 1500 to the late twentieth century.

- He surveyed political and economic data from 1500 onward, but avoided making predictions or creating a theory.

- The roots of *Rise and Fall* can be found in debates between the German historian Oswald Spengler* and the Canadian American historian William McNeill.* While they were not contemporaries, both made arguments about the ultimate future of the West.

Author's Aims

Paul Kennedy opens *The Rise and Fall of the Great Powers* with an unambiguous statement of intent. He says he aims "to trace and explain how the various Great Powers have risen and fallen, relative to each other," in terms of power, influence, and global importance, "over the five centuries," in Europe.[1]

Why five centuries? Why only Europe? After all, there have been "great powers" outside this time period, such as the Roman Empire.* There have also been non-European great powers, such as China during the Ming dynasty* of 1368–1644, but Kennedy does not concern himself with these. He chose to begin with the year 1500, he notes, because it marked the beginning of the "transoceanic, global system of states." And he chose to center his study on Europe, because the states on that continent would come to define the way in which that transoceanic global system worked.[2]

Kennedy makes much of Europe's peculiar geography in

> 66 The problem which historians—as opposed to political scientists—have in grappling with general theories is that the evidence of the past is almost always too varied to allow for 'hard' scientific conclusions. 99
>
> Paul Kennedy, *The Rise and Fall of the Great Powers*

explaining why Europe eventually became the "center of the world," politically speaking. Rivers, mountains, and forests divide the territories of Europe. These natural demarcations led to the natural emergence of many centers of power and these centers would vie for dominance. In this competitive system, the societies most able to fight and rule would prevail.[3]

Military might was not the only factor, but it was certainly the most important. After the voyage of the Italian explorer Columbus* in 1492 opened up the possibility of conquest abroad, Europe pulled ahead materially from other societies. A Spanish Austrian family—the Habsburgs*—threatened to become the predominant power in Europe; a coalition of European states dashed these hopes after a full 150 years of intermittent fighting.[4] Importantly, the Habsburg dynasty was not a state but a family whose alliances gave it hereditary control over a range of constantly shifting areas of Europe. Still, whether soldiers shed their blood for a state or for a family—whether they were fighting for territory or fighting to uphold personal bonds of loyalty—the war carried the same human and economic costs.

Approach

Kennedy's approach embraces a wide range of information and techniques of looking at information. *Rise and Fall* "concerns itself a great deal with wars ... but it is not strictly a book about military history." At the same time, while it is concerned with the evolution of the global economy, it is equally "not a work of economic history."[5] It gives us a synthesis of the actions of statesmen and the (economic) forces they brought to bear in working with (and against) one another.

Kennedy notes that a historian might understand his approach as "a broad and yet reasonably detailed survey" of great power politics, explained with reference to slow economic and technological changes. A political scientist might read the book as an exercise in theory-making—the theory being that we can predict the performance of great powers by looking at economic trends. But Kennedy is suspicious of such activity. Rather than making a predictive theory, he aims at "making sense of" past events. To put it crudely, money does not necessarily equal success, but "the power position of the leading nations has closely paralleled their relative economic position over the past five centuries." Kennedy believes it might be worthwhile to speculate how this could play out in future—but he hesitates to offer a prediction or make any claims to scientific precision.[6]

Contribution in Context

Kennedy was hardly alone in trying to write a "big" history of the West. In his 1922 book *The Decline of the West*, the German historian Oswald Spengler asked, "Is there a logic of history?"[7] Spengler argued that we should use "cultures" (such as the West) to analyze history, and we should see those cultures as having natural life cycles, from birth to death. Spengler defined cultures by the "prime symbols" that represent their main project. In his view, the "symbol" for Western culture is the character of Dr. Faustus,* a figure from German folklore dating back to at least the sixteenth century; according to the story, Faustus sold his soul to the devil in return for unlimited knowledge. Western society is "Faustian" because humanity has sold its soul and connection to the land for technical sophistication and industrial production. Cultures, over time, become civilizations, and increasingly focus on outward expansion. Spengler associates civilization with decline, since civilization represents the moment when the culture stops innovating and turns instead to expansion.

In response to Spengler's cyclical, pessimistic view, twentieth-century Canadian American historian William McNeill wrote *The Rise of the West*. In this 1962 work, McNeill argued that we should not see history as a series of cycles that different cultures progress through independently. Instead, "the principal factor promoting historically significant social change is contact with strangers possessing new and unfamiliar skills." As he sees it, civilization in general—and Western civilization in particular—possesses a uniquely high concentration of skills.[8] Civilizations remain separate, but the exchanges between them define their life cycles.

Taking a view almost entirely opposite to Spengler, McNeill believed that the West assured its dominance when it gained seafaring technology. This enabled the nations of Europe to become infinitely expansionist: "the result was to link the Atlantic face of Europe with the shores of most of the Earth." Europe "won" because it could adopt technologies and resources from everyone else at the expense of every other region.[9]

Both Spengler and McNeill focused on the relative position of the West with regard to other regions, telling a story of "rise and fall" similar to Kennedy's. Kennedy based his work on more ideas, however, with a focus on factors like technology or geography.

NOTES

1 Paul Kennedy, *The Rise and Fall of the Great Powers* (New York: Vintage Books, 1989), xv.

2 Kennedy, *Rise and Fall*, xv.

3 Kennedy, *Rise and Fall,* 30.

4 Kennedy, *Rise and Fall*, 31.

5 Kennedy, *Rise and Fall*, xv.

6 Kennedy, *Rise and Fall*, xxiv.

7 Oswald Spengler, *The Decline of the West*, ed. Helmut Warner, trans. Charles F. Atkinson (Oxford: Oxford University Press, 1991), 3.

8 William McNeill, "*The Rise of the West* After Twenty-five Years," *Journal of World History* 1, no. 1 (1990): 2.

9 William McNeill, *The Rise of the West: A History of the Human Community* (Chicago: Chicago University Press, 1991), 564–5.

SECTION 2
IDEAS

MAIN IDEAS

KEY POINTS

- While no one has created a formal definition of a "great power," the term commonly denotes a state recognized by its peers as capable of holding its own against any other in a military contest.

- Great powers fall when their military commitments exceed their productive capacity. Great powers rise when they build their military and productive capacity relative to those of other states.

- Although *Rise and Fall* contains no complex mathematics or academic jargon, its length can intimidate some readers.

Key Themes

At heart, Paul Kennedy's *The Rise and Fall of the Great Powers* aims to answer the question of what makes a state a "great power." We may define the term in two ways. The simple definition holds that a great power is a state that can reasonably defeat any other power in combat; the more social definition holds that a great power is a state that other states recognize as a great power. So the status of "great power" remains more a matter of mutual recognition than the passing of some arbitrary threshold.

The "great powers" Kennedy concerns himself with are, initially, dynasties centered on Spain, France, and Austria. Later in the book, he examines new entrants to the "Great Power Club"—including Russia, Great Britain, and Germany, among others.

For Kennedy, "all of the major shifts in the world's military-power balances"—meaning the relative strength of sovereign states—"have

> ❝ "While it would be quite wrong ... to claim that the outcome of the First World War was predetermined, the evidence presented here suggests that the overall course of that conflict—the early stalemate between the two sides, the ineffectiveness of the Italian entry, the slow exhaustion of Russia, the decisiveness of American intervention ... correlates closely with the economic and industrial production and effectively mobilized forces available to each alliance during the different phases of the struggle." ❞
>
> Paul Kennedy, *The Rise and Fall of the Great Powers*

followed alterations in the productive balances."[1] While his conclusion appears to be that victory follows wealth, it is not so simple; great powers make mistakes, even if they have significant resources. More often than not, then, great power conflicts can be prolonged and bloody, even if victory usually goes to the more prosperous of the two powers in conflict.

Exploring the Ideas

The first "rise and fall" Kennedy discusses is that of the Habsburg Empire, whose story unfolds between 1516 and 1689. In 1516, the Habsburg dynasty celebrated the coronation of Charles as Carlos I, King of Spain. In addition, through his ancestors, he was also Charles V,* leader of the Holy Roman Empire*—a political body that encompassed large parts of Austria, the Netherlands, Naples, and other territories around Europe. This "empire" was not a centralized authority like a state; it remained an association of distant provinces ruled by a single family.

Looking at why the Habsburgs failed, Kennedy argues that despite the enormous wealth from their holdings in Europe and the New

World (Spain's territories in South America), the Habsburgs could not afford to fight wars on many fronts over 140 years. They built their own warships rather than use trade ships, they maintained internal and external trade barriers, and they expelled Jews from their territories.[2] In short, the Habsburgs failed "to recognize the importance of preserving the economic underpinnings of a powerful military machine."

This revealed to Kennedy an important lesson: "the manufacturer and the farmer were as important as the cavalry officer and the pikeman."[3] A state must maintain enough productive capacity to fund its military commitments.

A great power fell, then, as a consequence of neglecting financial matters. In its wake, five great powers arose: Great Britain, the remains of the Habsburg Empire (Austria-Hungary), Prussia (a territory today incorporated into northern Germany), France, and Russia mounted the stage. Kennedy points to the "military revolution" of the time, as European states equipped, paid, and directed large, professional standing volunteer armies in Europe.[4]

Geography and finance, Kennedy writes, are factors of comparable importance.[5] Maintaining a professional army in peacetime required the state to borrow from financial markets. Great powers had to consider all the possible geographic fronts from which an invader could launch an attack. Given these circumstances, states that raised extensive funds to become "great powers" and fight one another fanned the flames of their own growth, pumping money into their own industries to house, equip, and train their military.

The historian John Brewer* calls this phenomenon the "fiscal-military state" and notes its characteristics as "high taxes, a growing and well-organized civil administration, a standing army, and the determination to act as a major … power."[6] In essence, the strongest fiscal position supports the strongest military position. As Kennedy puts it, no battlefield blunder was "enough to cancel out the advantages which that [combatant] possessed in terms of trained manpower, supply, organization, and economic base."[7]

This logic pervades Kennedy's exploration of history. As he points out in his assessment of World War I* (1914–18), the victorious powers enjoyed "a marked superiority in productive forces" after the United States joined the war in 1917. This "marked superiority," however, does not only reflect the quantity of available resources; it also reflects how those resources get deployed.

Kennedy discusses Germany's Hindenburg Programme,* a program intended to double the production of munitions. Germany made a "massive infrastructural investment" in new industrial resources such as blast furnaces for gun-making. But accomplishing this required the country to redirect all of its skilled labor, and to allow its other industrial and agricultural output to succumb to chronic neglect.[8] In the end, Germany's loss stemmed as much from neglecting its economic diversity as it did from any external military force.

Similarly, Kennedy's account of the end of World War II* shows that the "middle powers" (Britain, France, Germany) exhausted themselves, both by maintaining far-flung empires and by engaging in a grinding total war against one another. They followed this well-worn path to decline,[9] leaving the Americans and the Russians as the world's two dominant opposing powers.

Language and Expression

While Kennedy's subject, not to mention the length of the book, may be intimidating for some readers, his prose is clear and free of jargon. He illustrates his argument with tables such as that comparing the money spent on armaments between 1940 and 1943 and the money spent on either side of World War II. The simple charts supplement the text itself; the reader does not need to do any mathematics.[10]

Kennedy organizes his book chronologically, devoting much of the book to an overview of military actions (including wars lasting over a century) and economic and technological developments. These things actually constitute the "stuff" of history—the events we seek to explain.

Finally, he offers much more explanation and many more examples in the appendices; the reader will do well to follow each chapter through its endnotes, where he places many illustrative quotes from historical figures and useful bibliographic information.

NOTES

1 Paul Kennedy, *The Rise and Fall of the Great Powers* (New York: Vintage Books, 1989), 439.

2 Kennedy, *Rise and Fall*, 55.

3 Kennedy, *Rise and Fall*, 72.

4 M. Roberts, "The Military Revolution, 1560–1600," in *Essays in Swedish History*, ed. M. Roberts (London: Weidenfeld & Nicolson, 1967), 217.

5 Kennedy, *Rise and Fall*, 76.

6 John Brewer, *The Sinews of Power: War, Money, and the English State 1688–1783* (London: Century Hutchinson, 1988), 137.

7 Kennedy, *Rise and Fall*, 192.

8 Kennedy, *Rise and Fall*, 270.

9 Kennedy, *Rise and Fall*, 366–7.

10 Kennedy, *Rise and Fall*, 335.

MODULE 6
SECONDARY IDEAS

KEY POINTS

- The shifting balances between the great powers of the sixteenth to twentieth centuries set the stage for a new kind of competition in the second half of the twentieth century.

- The Cold War* was defined by its two opposing poles led by the United States and the Soviet Union,* the competing ideologies of communism* and capitalism,* and the threat of nuclear war—but its underlying dynamics remained economic.

- Kennedy's argument that the United States was in decline rested on the premise that the country's global commitments outmatched its capability to meet them; critics did not universally accept this viewpoint.

Other Ideas

In *The Rise and Fall of the Great Powers*, Paul Kennedy both explores the dynamics underlying the shifting balance of powers at the international level and, importantly, examines the roots of the international system of the twentieth century. The book's second major argument is that the dynamic of uneven economic growth "has had crucial long-term impacts" on the modern state system.[1]

The twentieth-century system was the result of two world wars that themselves resulted from jockeying for power among the five great powers of the eighteenth and nineteenth centuries. "It was becoming clear [in the aftermath of World War II]* that the global balance of power ... would be totally different from that preceding it."[2] France, Italy, and Germany were decimated by war; Japan (the first

> ❝ It was the United States alone which at this time had the productive and technological resources not only to wage two large-scale conventional wars but also to invest the scientists, raw materials, and money (about $2 billion) in the development of a new weapon [the atomic bomb] which might or might not work. The devastation inflicted upon Hiroshima, together with Berlin's fall into the hands of the Red Army, not only symbolized the end of another war, it also marked the beginning of a new order in world affairs. ❞
>
> Paul Kennedy, *The Rise and Fall of the Great Powers*

non-European great power) had lost its bid for mastery of Asia. Even the United Kingdom, which emerged from the war relatively better off than its European neighbors, could not compete with the rising powers of the United States and the Soviet Union.

In addition to exploring the roots and dynamics of the multipolar* international system in Europe (a system in which many nations were competing for supremacy), Kennedy discusses how these dynamics resulted in the emergence of the bipolar* international system between 1945 and 1991 (a system in which two nations vied for dominance). But Kennedy remains most interested in discussing how the US—in its Cold War bipolar contest with Russia from 1945 to 1991 and after—may follow old patterns and find itself in decline.

Exploring the Ideas

The end of World War II in 1945 left the Soviet Union and the United States facing one another in Europe. Joseph Stalin,* the General Secretary of the Soviet Communist Party (the Soviet Union's highest political office), consolidated control over Eastern Europe. He also pushed his armies into Central Asia, while "maintaining a high level of military security … to deter future aggressors" and keep its future conquests from falling into the American sphere of influence.*[3] In contrast, the United States attempted to enjoy what it called a global "Pax Americana."* Although the term refers to peace and prosperity under American rule, it disguises a great deal of internal violence in developing countries of the southern hemisphere. Kennedy believes the term references the "Pax Britannica"* of the late nineteenth century, a time of relative stability when Britain's "productive power and world influence" were predominant.[4] But two things made this twentieth-century global contest between great powers fundamentally different from its predecessors: the role of ideology and nuclear weapons.

Both blocs remained committed to their respective ideologies. The United States and its allies espoused liberal democratic capitalism (a system in which personal liberty is valued, elections are held, and industry and resources are held in private hands); the Soviet Union and its satellites practiced totalitarian* communism* (a system in which citizens are expected to be obedient to the state, which owns and manages industry and resources and in which property is held in common). Harry S. Truman,* president of the United States between 1945 and 1953, declared that "the United States … [helps] free people to maintain their institutions and their integrity against aggressive movements that seek to impose upon them totalitarian regimes." In other words, he vowed to prevent Soviet communism from expanding to new countries.[5]

In earlier eras, states would fight on a religious basis, or for abstract "national interests." However, the Cold War antagonists genuinely saw international affairs as a global struggle between good and evil and unlike previous great power standoffs, the entire world had a stake in the outcome of this one as the great powers had amassed arsenals of nuclear weapons.[6] Both the United States and Soviet Union had the means to eradicate all life on Earth at the push of a button.

Grand rhetoric—language intended to persuade or inflame—surrounded the Cold War. Kennedy's analysis of the conflict rests on the same logic as his analyses of previous great power struggles. It comes down to industry and economy rather than military. In the course of the Cold War, it became clear that the USSR's military and nuclear prowess "was not matched by parallel achievements at the economic level," especially in terms of technological innovation.[7] Kennedy hesitates to predict the future of international politics (in doing so he would leave history and enter the realm of political theory) but he does reiterate that "without a rough balance between these competing demands of defense, consumption, and investment, a Great Power is unlikely to preserve its status for long."[8]

Overlooked

After Kennedy had substantially completed the book, he decided to add some chapters dealing with the modern-day United States. The argument he makes in this section, which does not necessarily pertain to his main theory, has been perhaps the *most* discussed portion of the book: the United States, he reasons, is in relative decline. The US, like "Imperial Spain around 1600 or the British Empire around 1900," must deal with foreign military commitments that it has made in previous decades.[9]

Kennedy suggests that the United States may run the risk of imperial overreach; "decision-makers in Washington must face the awkward and enduring fact that the sum total of the United States' global interests and obligations is nowadays far larger than the country's power to defend them all simultaneously."[10] For Kennedy, American decline would be analogous to British decline in the nineteenth century.

Kennedy notes that declining *relative* economic performance underpins this overreach. While the United Stated carried less debt than it had relative to the rest of the world at the end of World War II, the country's Gross National Product* or GNP (the market value of all goods and services produced in one year by the residents of a country) and its manufacturing and agricultural output were declining.[11] Yet, simultaneously, US commitments abroad increased, with a corresponding pressure on the nation to spend more on its military.

While critics did not exactly overlook this argument, it was not central to Kennedy's project. One early critic—the American conservative political analyst Samuel Huntington*—believes Kennedy's theory that imperial overreach leads to decline may be true. But Huntington does not believe this necessarily applies to the US. For him, Kennedy's declinist* thesis rests too strongly on the assumption that economic power comes from similar sources. Huntington believes "the central sources of American strength" are competition through capitalism, social mobility, and renewal of culture and thought through immigration and universities. Kennedy, he believes, sees strength as coming from simple productive power measured in bushels of wheat or industrial output.[12]

NOTES

1 Paul Kennedy, *The Rise and Fall of the Great Powers* (New York: Vintage Books, 1989), 439.

2 Kennedy, *Rise and Fall*, 357.

3 Kennedy, *Rise and Fall*, 363.

4 Kennedy, *Rise and Fall*, 192.

5 Kennedy, *Rise and Fall*, 372.

6 Kennedy, *Rise and Fall*, 370.

7 Kennedy, *Rise and Fall*, 429.

8 Kennedy, *Rise and Fall*, 446.

9 Kennedy, *Rise and Fall*, 515.

10 Kennedy, *Rise and Fall*, 515.

11 Kennedy, *Rise and Fall*, 529.

12 Samuel Huntington, "The US: Decline or Renewal?" *Foreign Affairs* 67, no. 2 (1988): 89.

MODULE 7
ACHIEVEMENT

KEY POINTS

- Some critics questioned Kennedy's theories on the relationship between economics and power. They believe that by focusing on one factor alone, he lost the ability to explain outcomes that resulted from other factors.

- While *Rise and Fall* did not offer any predictions of how the Cold War* would end, overreach certainly played a role; the idea that something similar might happen to the United States in the future struck a nerve.

- Critics believe Kennedy's analysis was limited because his assumptions applied to European states; for them, he excluded non-European states from great power status by holding them to standards defined by Europe.

Assessing The Argument

Considering Paul Kennedy's *The Rise and Fall of the Great Powers*, certain questions remain difficult to answer. For example: does the book provide a useful explanatory model for understanding the peculiar history of "great power politics"? Does it explain why events unfolded the way they unfolded, without straying into the realm of prediction?

Although the Australian academic J. L. Richardson* thinks Kennedy's unwillingness to predict is "commendably modest and open ended," he finds his conclusions to be "disappointingly meagre." Richardson notes that Kennedy does not explain how states form coalitions, or how they identify their friends and enemies.[1] Second, Richardson recognizes that Kennedy has done great work analyzing the relationship between economic growth and war but he feels

> **❝** The end of the Cold War brought about nothing less than the collapse of an international system, something that has happened in modern history only once before. **❞**
>
> John Lewis Gaddis, "International Relations Theory and the End of the Cold War"

Kennedy did not necessarily finish his argument. "The economically strongest coalition wins," Richardson writes, admittedly oversimplifying Kennedy's conclusion. "[B]ut why were there particular coalitions formed in the first place? Why did great wars take place when they did, while at other times wars remained limited or were avoided altogether? ... Kennedy's work provokes questions of this kind but offers little to answer them."[2]

Essentially, Richardson's critique is that Kennedy can explain history *only as it happened*. He cannot account for wars averted, only wars that were waged. Are we left with a "history of great power politics," or a device that merely explains wars in which great powers have engaged? For Richardson, the work suffers by treating individual statesmen as relatively unimportant "relevant units of analysis," compared to broad-based economic, strategic, administrative, and technical shifts.[3]

Achievement in Context

Rise and Fall was published in 1987. According to Kennedy's Yale colleague John Lewis Gaddis,* a notable historian in his own right, the work seized the American national consciousness because it highlighted that "the condition of being a great power is in fact transitory," and may prove transitory for the United States as well.[4] Moreover, Kennedy suggested that the Cold War's end would not be peaceful. Gaddis cites Kennedy's conclusion: war has always accompanied the collapse of a great power empire, and those "who rejoice at the present-day difficulties of the Soviet Union* and who look forward to the collapse of that empire might wish to recall that such transformations normally occur at very great cost."[5]

But in this case, history did not repeat itself. The end of the Cold War and collapse of the Soviet Union occurred in relative peace. The Warsaw Pact*—the treaty of cooperation that had bound communist states together—officially dissolved in 1989. Lacking the guarantee of Soviet support against uprisings, unpopular communist leaders across Eastern Europe found themselves deposed in rapid sequence. This left the United States as the only surviving great power.

While Kennedy did not predict *how* the Cold War would end, he did understand that it would end. And according to one popular strand of thinking, its end did seem to mirror Kennedy's theory: by increasing defense spending in the United States, Ronald Reagan* (president between 1981 and 1989) forced the Soviet Union to make unsustainably large expenditures on its own military. The Soviets had also overextended themselves with overseas military commitments. These factors undermined the Soviet economy's ability to sustain itself. Additionally, we should note that Reagan's military spending did raise the US national deficit (the difference between its spending and its income) at the expense of the kind of "productive base" Kennedy believes is important.[6]

Some scholars disagree with this assessment, however. The American political scientist Richard Ned Lebow* and the Canadian international relations expert Janice Gross Stein* believe the arms build-up prolonged the Cold War. In their view, the conflict only ended once the leaders of the United States and Soviet Union met face to face and learned to trust one another as people.[7]

Limitations

The British historian Jeremy Black* suggests a difficulty with Kennedy's approach to the discipline, finding the same challenge with other Western historians who work on a "grand" level; for him, the issue of identifying great powers is problematic.

Scholars usually define "great powers" as those that have a significant amount of industrial and financial power. Still, as in many exclusive clubs, a state cannot be admitted to the "great power" club unless other members recognize it as one of their own. Black argues that, by definition, this excludes non-Western states; indeed, the list of attributes required for a state to be a "great power" merely describes certain Western states. "Thus, Japan, and then China, in the twentieth century are considered" great powers, but only because they merit the definition on Western terms—"earlier they are ruled out."[8] In other words, anyone can play the great power game, but the West makes the rules.

Black believes other powers outside Europe—such as the thirteenth-century Eurasian Mongol Empire*—would have been considered great powers if Kennedy had not loaded his premises in favor of European states. Black suggests other possible measures of great power status, such as honor and prestige—even if unconnected to financial or military resources. Without considerations like honor, Black writes, "it is difficult to explain why Austria, which he refers to as becoming a 'marginal first-class power' … from the eighteenth century" continued to receive such status, given its relative lack of material resources.[9]

NOTES

1   J. L. Richardson, "Paul Kennedy and International Relations Theory: A Comparison with Robert Gilpin," *Australian Journal of International Affairs* 45, no. 1 (1991): 75.

2   Richardson, "Paul Kennedy and International Relations Theory," 76.

3   Richardson, "Paul Kennedy and International Relations Theory," 76.

4   John Lewis Gaddis, "International Relations Theory and the End of the Cold War," *International Security* 17, no. 3 (1992): 50–1.

5   Paul Kennedy, *The Rise and Fall of the Great Powers* (New York: Vintage Books, 1989), 514.

6   Richard Ned Lebow and Janice Gross Stein, "Reagan and the Russians," *Atlantic Monthly*, February 1994, accessed September 12, 2015, http://www.theatlantic.com/past/politics/foreign/reagrus.htm.

7   Lebow and Stein, "Reagan and the Russians."

8   Jeremy Black, *Great Powers and the Quest for Hegemony: The World Order Since 1500*, (London: Routledge, 2008), 1–2.

9   Black, *Great Powers*, 20.

MODULE 8
PLACE IN THE AUTHOR'S WORK

KEY POINTS

- *Rise and Fall* served as the culmination of Kennedy's career looking at grand diplomatic history.

- Kennedy focused his work initially on high politics, and later on global governance.

- *Rise and Fall* remains most famous for its discussion of American decline; for this reason, Kennedy remains an influential academic and popular figure.

Positioning

The Rise and Fall of the Great Powers was not Paul Kennedy's first significant book—or even his first to be titled *Rise and Fall*. Kennedy called his first prominent work, published in 1976, *The Rise and Fall of British Naval Mastery*. This reflects his early fascination with ways in which the British Empire* balanced its power on land and sea. In his later work, Kennedy would continue to explore one key element of *British Naval Mastery*: Britain's global influence and prosperity did not stem from the strength of its navy. In fact, the relationship ran the other way around.[1] Britain's domestic economy remains crucial to its ability to project its force at sea.

Kennedy published another similarly titled and significant work, *The Rise of the Anglo-German Antagonism: 1860–1914*, in 1980. Like Kennedy's other books, *Antagonism* dealt with all levels of political life, especially international diplomacy and domestic politics. In it, as in his other works, he advances the theory that "the most profound cause [of Anglo-German tension] … was economic."[2] Germany's political unification and economic growth in the nineteenth century indicated that the nation was heading towards socialism* (a political system in

> ❝ If the immediate fallout was hard to deal with, the longer-term consequences have proved positive. The book became an international bestseller and has been translated into 23 languages; only last year the Chinese issued a reprint to coincide with a new 10-part TV series based on it. ❞
>
> John Crace, "Paul Kennedy: Neocons' Worst Nightmare," *The Guardian*

which industry and resources are held in the hands of the people), especially as elements of the population campaigned to make domestic politics more democratic. The ruling elite responded with a strategy called *Weltpolitik*,* which aimed at fostering intense national pride and increasing German military power to make it a great power, like its neighbors France, Germany, and Russia. Essentially, *Weltpolitik* ("world policy") is tough diplomacy, in which a risen Germany, having attained parity with its European neighbors, seeks to install itself as a "great power" with an empire, a strong navy, and tough-talking diplomacy.

Integration

Kennedy's early body of work remains relatively well integrated. By the time *Rise and Fall* appeared in 1987, scholars had written a great deal about how economic prosperity (or lack thereof) connected to political outcomes. After *Rise and Fall*, Kennedy branched out, expanding both his subject and his purpose.

In 1993's *Preparing for the 21st Century*, Kennedy examines transnational forces—rather than the "nation-state"—as the main unit of analysis. He expects that population growth, resource scarcity, environmental damage, and a globally widening wealth-gap will fundamentally undermine the power of the nation-state. For him, the nation-state was a European institution, and too insular to deal with global problems.[3] The only way to deal with these interlocking problems, he maintains, is to make leadership more transnational.

In *The Parliament of Man*, published in 2006, Kennedy continues the pessimistic discussion he began in *Preparing*. But this time he has a solution in mind: the United Nations,* a global institution founded to promote cooperation between nations. True, the United Nations has problems of its own. It cannot create authoritative rules, and it still largely respects the sovereignty of nation-states but in theory the UN provides humanity's best chance of coordinating a genuine global response to transnational problems that defy national solutions. The American international relations scholar John Ikenberry* writes that in *Parliament of Man* Kennedy focuses on how the UN's role in "supporting social and political advancements" or "peacekeeping and the promotion of human rights" has produced some success. Humanity has a fighting chance for survival if we can deepen these victories.[4]

Ultimately, the objects of Kennedy's previous study—the great powers—have a role to play in these new studies but they pose a fundamental problem in their "uncertain and often fleeting ability … to work together."[5]

Significance

Having apparently failed adequately to predict the imminent downfall of the Soviet Union, *Rise and Fall* may seem like a book of its time. Perhaps because Kennedy has since moved on to write about transnational issues, however, this earlier work retains a timeless relevance. While Kennedy wrote the final chapters of *Rise and Fall* as an addendum to the earlier chapters, it is this section of the work, with its discussion of the possibility of American decline, that people remember as most significant.

Although, as the British journalist John Crace* wrote, "Kennedy's new book, *The Rise and Fall of the Great Powers*, had touched a raw nerve," that had not been Kennedy's intention; as he told an interviewer: "It was actually a study of more than 500 years of global empires … but I don't think many people read more than the final chapter on the US and the USSR."[6]

The influential British financial periodical *The Economist** notes that Kennedy's thesis "looked premature"[7] because the work came out before the end of the Cold War.* However, by the turn of the millennium, with the United States' commitments in Iraq* and Afghanistan,* and a financial crisis in the early 2000s, "the picture starts to look rather like the one that led Professor Kennedy to make his premature judgment."[8]

Ultimately, Kennedy's book came to symbolize Americans' anxiety that their nation may, like great powers before it, fall into decline. Kennedy continues to wield national influence on this subject. Decades after the publication of his book, policymakers still consult him as an authority on American decline.

NOTES

1   Paul Kennedy, *The Rise and Fall of British Naval Mastery* (London: Allen Lane, 1976), 140.

2   Paul Kennedy, *The Rise of the Anglo-German Antagonism: 1860–1914* (London: George Allen & Unwin, 1980), 464.

3   Neal Acherson, "Interview with Paul Kennedy," *Independent,* March 28, 1993, accessed September 12, 2015, http://www.independent.co.uk/voices/interview–prepare-to-meet-thy-future-big-books-about-the-21st-century-are-supposed-to-make-your-flesh-creep-but-paul-kennedy-argues-that-the-end-of-the-world-is-not-quite-nigh-1500508.html.

4   John Ikenberry, "Review of *Parliament of Man*," *Foreign Affairs* 85, no. 6 (2006): 156.

5   Ikenberry, "Review," 156.

6   John Crace, "Paul Kennedy: Neocons' Worst Nightmare," *Guardian,* February 5, 2008, accessed September 3, 2015, http://www.theguardian.com/education/2008/feb/05/academicexperts.highereducationprofile.

7   "Imperial Overstretch?" *The Economist,* June 27, 2002, accessed September 12, 2015, http://www.economist.com/node/1188741.

8   *Economist,* "Imperial Overstretch?"

SECTION 3
IMPACT

MODULE 9
THE FIRST RESPONSES

KEY POINTS

- Critics accused Kennedy of making his theory too broad, and too full of assumptions that sidelined either domestic priorities or diplomatic maneuvering.

- Kennedy responded by suggesting that his critics oversimplified his theory and focused too much on the short term.

- The Cold War* ended four years after the publication of *Rise and Fall*. After that, critics fell into two camps: those who believed the United States would be the sole world power, and those who believed that international polarity* would shift from one power (unipolarity) to many powers (multipolarity).*

Criticism

Paul Kennedy's *The Rise and Fall of the Great Powers* quickly became a source of discussion—both critical and supportive. The American military strategist Edward Luttwak* suggests that Kennedy did not write the book as a "historian," but as a "publicist"[1] who set out with a theory in mind. Rather than trying to test this theory against other theories, Kennedy asserts (says Luttwak) that societies experience different rates of growth because they "just do." Luttwak notes, "he does not, for example, argue that comparable societies have different rates of growth because their societal priorities are different."[2]

The American political strategist Joseph Nye, Jr.* argued that, especially in the post-Cold War era, we need to reconceptualize power. Nye coined the phrase "soft power," which contrasts "to the hard command power usually associated with tangible resources like

> " Kennedy's predictions have not fared well over the past decade and more. Russia did indeed continue to decline, but not for the reasons Kennedy argued. Russia kept sinking even after it shed the burdens of the Soviet empire and military interventions in Afghanistan and elsewhere. The other powers that Kennedy predicted would decline did not decline at all. The United States experienced a spectacular rebirth, not only 'winning' the Cold War but becoming once again the dominant economic power in the world. "
>
> Henry R. Nau, "Why *The Rise and Fall of the Great Powers* Was Wrong"

military and economic strength." Soft power convinces rather than compels.[3] Examples of soft power include technology, popular culture, and leadership in international institutions. When the world listens to American pop music, the argument goes, the United States gains a kind of cultural legitimacy that rewards Americans with both money and influence. How does having globally important pop culture lead to power? "A country that stands astride popular channels of communication," Nye argues, "has more opportunities to get its messages across and to affect the preferences of others."[4] Nye's criticisms pointed out that Kennedy might have overlooked some dimensions of power relevant in the present day.

The next thread of criticism focused on the link between power and economic prosperity. In a colorfully titled essay "Beware of Historians Bearing False Analogies," one American political theorist noted that "relative reduction in military outlays does not automatically translate into a higher growth rate."[5] The American professor of international affairs Charles Kupchan* takes this argument further, citing the decline of the British Empire* in the early twentieth century; Britain's economic predominance was dropping "not because of excessive military expenditure" (in fact, military expenses were decreasing) but "because of rapid economic growth in other countries and the failure of British industry to adapt to technological change."[6] In the twentieth century, newly industrializing states with regional rivals, such as Taiwan* or South Korea,* enjoy "high rates of growth while maintaining relatively high levels of military spending."[7] Kupchan believes military spending *can* damage the economy, but it can also help the economy—new technologies often emerge from military research, for example. He concludes that the relationship Kennedy suggests is ill defined, and may merely be one of many possible relationships.

Responses

Kennedy suggests that Luttwak has oversimplified his theory. Yes, great powers became overextended and exhausted, and fell but this remains "an accompanying cause, not the central factor" of why states enjoy varying levels of power and influence.[8] Kennedy presents a more nuanced version of this argument. Great powers (including the United States) show "a very significant correlation *over the longer term* between productive and revenue-raising capacities on the one hand and military strength on the other."[9]

More important to the concept of overreach, Kennedy identifies a lag time between a power's economic decline and its military decline. When a state faces decline, strategic commitments will naturally take precedence over economic capacity. This hastens the fall.[10] Essentially, the two forces interact mutually: economic decline precedes overreach, overreach makes economic recovery more difficult. Toward the end of the Cold War, even if American military spending had shrunk *in absolute terms*, it still remained higher relative to the United States' current economic prosperity, which can be problematic—a counter-argument that also applies to Kupchan.

Kupchan criticized Kennedy for over-generalizing and for

imagining too simplistic a relationship between economic and military factors. Imperial overreach and economic decline, Kennedy argued, frequently go hand in hand; it was not that military spending is directly correlated to economic decline.

Conflict and Consensus

The Cold War ended just four years after *Rise and Fall* was published. It is generally agreed that the world then entered a "unipolar" phase, meaning that the United States was the only major world power. This position, first outlined by American political commentator Charles Krauthammer,* holds that "the immediate post-Cold War world is not multipolar ... The center of world power is an unchallenged superpower, the United States, attended by its Western allies."[11] Essentially, it appeared to Krauthammer and others that, far from declining due to imperial overreach, the United States would not only continue to be *a* great power, it would be the *only* great power, as no states could challenge its position. There were, roughly, two positions: either American power would decline or the country would remain alone as a superpower.

The American political scientist Henry Nau* took issue with Kennedy's predictions about American decline after the end of the Cold War. In his provocatively titled essay "Why *The Rise and Fall of the Great Powers* Was Wrong," Nau argued that Kennedy had ignored the impact of identity and domestic politics. For Nau, history is not the story of great powers rising and falling. In his view, "democratic powers succeed best in creating wealth and power," reducing the need for military competition and creating greater peace (and productivity) among all states.[12] Essentially, Nau suggested that the United States' democratic, capitalist* system, with elections and private wealth, made it less prone to decline than previous great powers. The United States' political and economic systems could break the pattern of decline Kennedy found inevitable. Kennedy did not respond directly to Nau's argument, but rather suggested that "his predictions might be more appropriately assessed after another decade or so"—that is, around 2010.[13]

NOTES

1   Paul Kennedy and Edward Luttwak, "*The Rise and Fall of the Great Powers*: An Exchange," *American Scholar* 59, no. 2 (1990): 287.

2   Kennedy and Luttwak, "*The Rise and Fall of the Great Powers*," 289.

3   Joseph Nye, Jr., "The Changing Nature of World Power," *Political Science Quarterly* 105, issue 2 (1990): 181.

4   Joseph Nye, Jr., "Soft Power," *Foreign Policy* no. 80 (1990): 169.

5   W. W. Rostow, "Beware of Historians Bearing False Analogies," *Foreign Affairs* 66, no. 4 (1988): 868.

6   Charles Kupchan, "Empire, Military Power, and Economic Decline," *International Security* 13, no. 4 (1989): 42.

7   Kupchan, "Empire, Military Power," 45.

8   Kennedy and Luttwak, "*The Rise and Fall of the Great Powers*," 285.

9   Kennedy and Luttwak, "*The Rise and Fall of the Great Powers*," 285.

10 Kennedy and Luttwak, "*The Rise and Fall of the Great Powers*," 285.

11 Charles Krauthammer, "The Unipolar Moment," *Foreign Affairs* 70, no. 1 (1990/91): 23.

12 Henry Nau, "Why *The Rise and Fall of the Great Powers* Was Wrong," *Review of International Studies* 27, no. 4 (2001): 592.

13 Nau, "Why *The Rise and Fall of the Great Powers* Was Wrong," 580.

MODULE 10
THE EVOLVING DEBATE

KEY POINTS

- The question of the United States' decline remains open, even after the terrorist attacks of September 11, 2001 ("9/11")* and the problems arising from the "War on Terror"* (the United States' military operations in the Middle East and Africa against terrorist organizations).

- The term "big history"* refers to the study of history that analyzes one major concept or category over a long time period.

- The Indian American writer Fareed Zakaria* may be the most important theorist of American decline today; for him, while the world is becoming "post-American," the United States' prestige might be preserved if the nation increased its toleration of others.

Uses And Problems

After Paul Kennedy published *The Rise and Fall of the Great Powers* in 1987, the United States enjoyed seemingly unchallenged power throughout the 1990s, and his "decline" thesis fell out of fashion in the early years of the twenty-first century. In a remarkable about-face, Kennedy wrote in a 2002 *Financial Times** article that the United States has maintained its unipolar* hegemony*—that is, its dominance. He cautioned, however, that this role "very much rests upon a decade of impressive economic growth," and that loss of this growth might cause "the threat of overreach [to] return" as the country's military commitments increased after the terrorist attacks on US soil committed on September 11, 2001—the atrocities known as 9/11.[1]

In 2003, Kennedy, the American political strategist Joseph Nye,

> ❝ The most significant political phenomenon of our new century is going to be the relative rise of Asia, perhaps China especially, and its natural concomitant, the relative decline of the west as a whole and more particularly of both of its two greatest components, Europe and the US. ❞
>
> Paul Kennedy, *Rise and Fall of the Great Powers*

Jr.,* and the political consultant Richard Perle* participated in a symposium called "The Reluctant Empire." The panel primarily focused on how the United States should secure itself in a post-9/11 world, especially in light of the war in Iraq.* Recapitulating some of his economic argument, Kennedy suggested that a protracted war in Iraq would affect domestic prosperity but he spent most of his time talking about the consequences the war would have for the United States' "soft power."* Beyond the cost in civilian lives, he argued, the war would also reduce the influence of international organizations, because the US began the war unilaterally and without the authorization of the United Nations.*[2]

Kennedy did not confine his remarks here to the relationship between economics and strategy, as his discussion of the "soft power" consequences of the Iraq War shows. Ultimately, though, Kennedy believes the United States has allowed its security commitments to create a kind of "empire," since it wields "a global influence that is disproportionate to a country that has less than 5 percent of the world's population."[3]

After 9/11 ratcheted up the United States' quasi-imperial commitments abroad, the financial crisis of 2007–8 diminished economic resources at home—and Kennedy reaffirmed his belief in American decline once again. In an article for the US financial periodical the *Wall Street Journal*,* he argued, "The data so far suggest the economies of China and India are growing (not as fast as in the past but still growing), while America's economy shrinks in absolute terms."Because of that, the United States should not expect its share of total world production to remain at the height it reached in previous years.[4] He concludes that this situation heralds a "global tectonic power shift" westward across the Pacific, from America to Asia. It remains up to the government of the United States to handle that shift.

Schools of Thought

Rise and Fall may be considered a work of scholarship relevant to the disciplines of history and of political science. For Kennedy, it is a work of "big history,"* which he defines as "single-volume books whose authors took hold of a vast topic and then wrestled it to the ground, comprehended it, and explained it to readers."[5] In effect, "big history" represents a theorized approach to history that aims to explain some large category of event. In Kennedy's case, this category could be the relative strength of great powers. In the case of the Scottish historian Niall Ferguson,* another scholar in this genre and a similarly popular writer, the category would be the advent of global Western dominance—and the threat other states pose to that continued dominance. Ferguson suggests that in 1500 the notion that Western Europe would come to dominate the world "would have come to seem wildly fanciful." He asks "what was it about the civilization of Western Europe after the fifteenth century that allowed it to trump the outwardly superior empires of the Orient?"[6] Ferguson investigates the ascendancy of the West so "we can hope to estimate ... the imminence of our decline and fall."[7]

In Current Scholarship

Fareed Zakaria, perhaps the most important "declinist"* working today (that is, a proponent of the belief that the power and influence of the United States is waning), may be best known for his 2009 book

The Post-American World. He notes that "for the roughly two decades since 1989, the power of the United States has defined the international order," meaning the nation remained the only relevant political player. This stemmed from a complex mix of factors—economic, military, and the mere fact of being the only great power standing after the Cold War.*

Politics today has moved on though.[8] If the world continues to be defined by the United States' remaining—and waning—strength, "several other important great powers" such as China, Russia, or the European Union* must be factored into any analysis. Zakaria sees "greater assertiveness and activity from all actors."[9] Essentially, Zakaria argues, as US economic and military power declines relative to others, no other nation is attempting to supplant the United States. The truth is that the rising powers simply care about one another more. Zakaria sees the strength of the United States in its openness, and suggests that to keep the world from becoming too "post-American," the country must bolster its commitment to openness and tolerance.[10] In Zakaria's estimation, openness encourages the goodwill of others, harnesses the best abilities of the country's population, and attracts talent from abroad.

NOTES

1 Paul Kennedy, "The Eagle Has Landed," *Financial Times*, February 1, 2002.

2 Paul Kennedy et al., "The Reluctant Empire: In a Time of Great Consequence," *Brown Journal of World Affairs* 10, no. 1 (2003): 16.

3 Kennedy et al., "The Reluctant Empire," 16.

4 Paul Kennedy, "American Power is on the Wane," *Wall Street Journal*, January 1, 2009, accessed September 14, 2015, http://www.wsj.com/articles/SB123189377673479433.

5 Paul Kennedy, "The Distant Horizon: What Can 'Big History' Tell Us About America's Future?" *Foreign Affairs* 87, no. 3 (2008) : 126–7.

6 Niall Ferguson, *Civilization: The West and the Rest* (London: Allen Lane, 2010), 8.

7 Ferguson, *Civilization*, 18.

8 Fareed Zakaria, *The Post-American World* (New York: W.W. Norton and Company, 2008), 42.

9 Zakaria, *The Post-American World*, 43.

10 Zakaria, *The Post-American World*, 257.

MODULE 11
IMPACT AND INFLUENCE TODAY

KEY POINTS

- *Rise and Fall* remains best known for raising important questions about American decline, and how the United States should manage its own loss of hegemony* to China.

- Some argue that the United States should fight its decline and accept its role as a global leader, as leadership delivers significant benefits (in terms of agenda-setting, soft power,* and economic returns) relative to its cost.

- Opponents argue that the benefits of global engagement do not outweigh the costs. They feel that the United States ought to reconsider and adopt a more sustainable role in international affairs.

Position

Paul Kennedy wrote *The Rise and Fall of the Great Powers* as a work of history, spanning the period from 1500 to the latter half of the twentieth century. For Americans concerned with national decline, it remains most relevant as a work of political science. Still, many international relations scholars today have become concerned more with the issue of hegemony than with pure power, and Kennedy's way of examining the international system seems less applicable.

Through his discussion of "world hegemony," the Italian political economist Giovanni Arrighi* provides an alternative to the notion of European "great power" competition; for him, it is "the power of a state to exercise functions of leadership and governance over a system of sovereign states."[1] For theorists of international history like Arrighi, the concept of "hegemony" became more interesting than that of "great power," as its roots lie in the capacity both to define

> ❝ In modern history, there have been two liberal
> international orders: *Pax Britannica* and *Pax Americana*. In
> building their respective international structures, Britain
> and the United States wielded their power to advance
> their own economic and geopolitical interests. But they
> also bestowed important benefits—public goods—on the
> international system as a whole. ❞
>
> Christopher Layne, "The End of the *Pax Americana*"

and rule the international system. These theorists would find it
meaningless to assume that great powers were a feature of Europe
alone. For them, Europeans exercise hegemonic control over the
rest of the world, defining the world system in their own image.

Rise and Fall does not play a defining role in the debate about the
ways in which the United States should conduct itself. Instead, as the
most important statement of the thesis that the United States is in
decline, it raises questions "about the structural, fiscal and economic
weaknesses in America that, over time, could nibble away at the
foundations of US power."[2] The 1990s delivered a period of
unprecedented growth and international esteem, causing some to
dismiss predictions of decline. According to the American scholar
Christopher Layne,* in the wake of the financial crisis* of 2007–8,
the theory gained new traction.[3] A landmark study by the Brookings
Institution*—an influential body that aims to influence US foreign
policy—attributes the source of "relative decline" to the rise of
China. China's regional power has increased, in no small part
facilitated by explosive economic growth. This growth, in turn, has
fueled an expansion of China's military capability.[4] The Brookings
report defines the relationship between China and the United States
as "strategic distrust"—a perception that "the other side will seek to
achieve its key long term goals at concerted cost to your own side's

core prospects and interests."[5]

Interaction

Kennedy said that dominant countries face dilemmas as they decline—specifically a reduction in economic strength and growing strategic commitments abroad. To preserve prestige in the face of these dilemmas, is it better to allocate more funds to the military, or pull back?[6] In a 2013 article called "Lean Forward," the American scholars Stephen Brooks,* John Ikenberry* and William Wohlforth* wrote, "Washington might be tempted to … pull back from the world. The rise of China is chipping away at the United States' preponderance of power [and] a budget crisis has put defense spending on the chopping block."[7] In light of this, they endorsed the notion of spending more on international commitments; as they explained it, the United States might be tempted to avoid "imperial overreach" by pulling back from its strategic commitments, and redress a growing rift between its power resources and economic resources. But as costly as the US's global commitments may be, they play a more central role in the nation's prosperity than we might imagine; in the authors' words, "military dominance undergirds its economic leadership."[8]

The global dominance of the United States allows the country to serve the common good in many important ways. The US Navy secures sea lanes. The US dollar serves as the world's reserve currency.* And the US offers its allies economic leverage in their military expenditures. Allies can maintain smaller defense budgets because the US has guaranteed their security both bilaterally and under the NATO pact.*[9] The US enjoys disproportionate gains from these expensive outlays because they help "prevent the outbreak of conflict in the world's most important regions, keep the global economy humming, and make international cooperation easier" for everyone, and allow the US to shape what the world looks like.[10]

The Continuing Debate

The American political scientist Barry Posen* wrote a companion piece to "Lean Forward," entitled "Pull Back." Posen agrees with Kennedy that the United States should have fewer global entanglements. In *Rise and Fall*, Kennedy had written, "The task facing American statesmen over the next decades is to recognize that broad trends are under way, and that there is a need to 'manage' affairs so that the *relative* erosion of the United States' position takes place slowly and smoothly."[11]

Posen argues that the US ought to manage its decline by slowly reducing the world's dependence on its generosity. For example, taking on the defense burdens of many European and Asian allies and entangling itself in conflicts abroad in order to further its international agenda brings with it consequences: it "makes enemies almost as fast as it slays them, discourages allies from paying for their own defense, and convinces powerful states to band together and oppose Washington's plans, further raising the costs of carrying out its foreign policy."[12]

Posen sees the United States as trying singlehandedly to maintain global security. While the US undertakes drawn-out occupations of failed states and maintains security agreements with Taiwan, Japan, and Europe, other states fail to shoulder the burden of global security. Posen argues for a "nimble" grand strategy, where states combat terrorism with "carefully applied force, rather than through wholesale nation-building efforts such as that in Afghanistan."[13] Essentially, "if the US debt keeps growing and power continues to shift to other countries, some future economic or political crisis could force Washington to switch course abruptly."[14] If the United States were to pull back rapidly, it would create a vacuum for other powers such as China to assume its leadership role.

NOTES

1   Giovanni Arrighi, *The Long Twentieth Century: Money, Power, and the Origins of Our Times* (London: Verso, 2002), 27.

2   Christopher Layne, "The End of the Pax Americana: How Western Decline Became Inevitable," *The Atlantic,* April 2012, accessed September 14, 2015, http://www.theatlantic.com/international/archive/2012/04/the-end-of-pax-americana-how-western-decline-became-inevitable/256388/.

3   Layne, "The End of the Pax Americana."

4   Kenneth Lieberthal and Wang Jisi, *Addressing US–China Strategic Distrust* (Washington, DC: Brookings Institution, 2012), 2–3.

5   Lieberthal and Jisi, *Addressing US–China Strategic Distrust,* 5.

6   Paul Kennedy, *The Rise and Fall of the Great Powers* (New York: Vintage Books, 1989), 533.

7   Stephen Brooks et al., "Lean Forward: In Defense of American Engagement," *Foreign Affairs* 92, no. 1 (2013): 116.

8   Brooks et al., "Lean Forward," 124.

9   Brooks et al., "Lean Forward," 124.

10 Brooks et al., "Lean Forward," 125.

11 Kennedy, *Rise and Fall*, 534.

12 Barry Posen, "Pull Back: The Case for a Less Activist Foreign Policy," *Foreign Affairs* 92, no. 1 (2013): 117.

13 Posen, "Pull Back," 122.

14 Posen, "Pull Back," 128.

MODULE 12
WHERE NEXT?

KEY POINTS

- Kennedy has recently argued that China is rising relative to the United States in both economic and military terms.

- The American lawyer and scholar Philip Bobbitt argued that war has changed in the twenty-first century. In the past, only states had the capacity to create mass violence. Today, technology has made it possible for smaller, less well-funded groups to wreak havoc.

- While *Rise and Fall* was important as a work of history, it is primarily remembered by and debated within the field of political science for its prediction that the United States would experience a decline following the Cold War.*

Potential

While *The Rise and Fall of the Great Powers* may be important as a work of international history, Paul Kennedy remains an active participant in the debate over how the United States will accommodate (or resist) the decline predicted in the book's final chapters. Kennedy points out that "Asia is growing at a significantly faster pace than the mature economies of the US and Europe," especially in terms of the balance of capital.[1] He notes that "surplus bank savings have usually accompanied the alterations in the military–political balances of power … from the Lombard cities to Antwerp and Amsterdam; from there to London; from London … to New York; and from New York … to where? Shanghai?" Simply put, Asia has increasingly become wealthier and financially more important than the West.

The military balance has also shifted, especially as it relates to sea power (which includes aircraft carriers). Kennedy thinks American

> **❝** We must urgently develop legal and strategic parameters for state action in the Wars against Terror. Ultimately this will be a matter of drawing the links between successfully warring on terror and evolving legal concepts of sovereignty and its relationship to lawful, legitimate governance. **❞**
>
> Philip Bobbitt, *Terror and Consent*

strategists must be asking, "Why is Beijing spending so much on defense?" Even if China's defense budget remains lower in absolute terms, it is growing relatively. "Why this heavy investment into cyber-warfare?; into military satellites?; into commercial espionage? What about those medium-range sea-skimming missiles that fly below the radar screens of US warships, and those ultra-long-range rockets that can cross the wide Pacific?"[2] If China's naval capabilities (and therefore, its ability to project power worldwide) are growing *relative* to the United States, is American domination of the Pacific Ocean not shrinking? The Pacific encompasses half the world. In *Rise and Fall*, Kennedy argues that power can be measured both financially and militarily. It seems that China's power is growing and the United States' shrinking; we may be witnessing the relative decline of a great power.

Future Directions

One prominent successor to Kennedy's project of discussing the United States' place in the world is Philip Bobbitt.* His books *The Shield of Achilles: War, Peace, and the Course of History* (2002) and *Terror and Consent: The Wars for the Twenty-first Century* (2008) both present a picture of history in which technological change, constitutional change, and economic change work together. Bobbitt notes that the "objective" of the wide-ranging "War on Terror"* being fought by the United States, largely in the Middle East and Africa, "is not the conquest of territory or the silencing of any particular ideology"—the kind of war Paul Kennedy might recognize. Instead, Bobbitt says it is "to secure the environment necessary for states of consent and to make it impossible for our enemies to impose or induce states of terror."[3]

Bobbitt identifies what he calls "states of consent"—Western states that depend on the consent of citizens for their legitimacy and see their primary job as protecting those civilians. The growth of technology and connectedness has enabled this protection to enter a new realm. Where is the threat? Bobbitt's assessment of the United States' strength in the face of this new kind of enemy stands in stark contrast to Kennedy's in *Rise and Fall*. The US has the world's largest economy. It supports "a large army equipped with infinitely superior weaponry and communications." But "the harm that can be done to the American nation is growing more quickly (as technology disperses and becomes cheaper) than its lead is increasing."[4]

In other words, Bobbitt believes technology has altered the dynamics Kennedy analyzed in the late twentieth century. The capacity to do large-scale violence used to be the exclusive province of states. And in part, the robustness of the economy defined this capacity; such violence required too many resources for entities other than nations to consider it. Today, in Bobbitt's view, military might and the economy have become less important than cohesiveness among states and forward planning in the face of terror. In effect, states will survive if they can remain networked with one another, and anticipate threats.

Summary

Paul Kennedy's *The Rise and Fall of the Great Powers* is first and foremost a work of history. Kennedy analyzes the powers that have really mattered in the world since 1500 and determines the factors that enabled these powers to rise to that level of prominence. He also warns of forces that might cause their prominence to fall. Despite the thorough historical analysis it contains, scholars remember *Rise and Fall* as a work of political science. Its final chapters, added almost as an afterthought, captured the fears of the time: that the United States might be a great power due to fall.

Kennedy argues that strategy and economics are intimately bound. A state rises to prominence because it enjoys relative growth and superior productive capacity. Kennedy measures this in industrial and agricultural production, the very basics of prosperity, rather than simple resource endowment. Economic prosperity enables the state to create a fighting force that can prevail in any battle and a "great power" is born. When the growing state overcommits—often, paradoxically, to protect material wealth—"imperial overreach" sets in. States will find themselves like an old man carrying a heavy burden up a hill: other powers with relatively more dynamic economies, and fewer foreign commitments soaking up resources from those economies, will catch up and outpace those slowing down.

This is not only a powerful (if very simple) paradigm* to understand history, it also served as a powerful warning to the United States that it must not move to create an "empire" of its own at the end of the Cold War. Otherwise, it would tread the well-worn path to decline, as have the other great powers in Kennedy's work.

NOTES

1 Paul Kennedy, "Asia's Rise: Rise and Fall," *The World Today* 66, no. 8/9 (2010): 7.

2 Kennedy, "Asia's Rise: Rise and Fall," 7.

3 Philip Bobbitt, *Terror and Consent: The Wars for the Twenty-first Century* (London: Penguin, 2009), 3.

4 Bobbitt, *Terror and Consent*, 537.

GLOSSARY

GLOSSARY OF TERMS

Aberystwyth University: a research University in Wales, in the United Kingdom.

Afghanistan War: a military conflict starting in 2001 in which a United States-led NATO coalition fought al-Qaeda and the Taliban.

Anarchy: a condition in which there is no administrative or governing authority to enforce rules.

Annales school: a French school of historical thought that emphasizes the long-term influences on day-to-day living, through interdisciplinary methods (methods that draw on the aims and methods of different academic disciplines, in this case geography, economics, and sociology). This contrasted with the more traditional way of studying history, which presented dramatic events in sequence.

Außenpolitik: a German term referring to "the politics of outside." It suggests that foreign policy is the most important activity pursued by states.

Big history: a theorized approach to history that aims to explain a large category or concept. The term is also used to describe the recently emerging study of the entire history of the universe from its beginnings in the big bang to the present.

Bipolar: an international order characterized by two opposing state powers.

British Empire (sixteenth to twentieth centuries): the areas of the world under direct control by Britain. After World War I, it comprised up to 25 percent of the world's land and 20 percent of its population. While the empire fell into serious decline in the aftermath of World War II, scholars generally mark its end as the return of Hong Kong to China in 1997.

Brookings Institution: an American think tank, considered the world's most influential, that aims to affect American foreign policy. In general, it supports a more open and interconnected international system.

Capitalism: an economic system that emphasizes private property rights and the pursuit of profit from privately owned industry.

Cold War (1947–91): a period of tension between the United States and the Soviet Union. While the two countries never engaged in direct military conflict, they were involved in covert and proxy wars and espionage against one another.

Communism: a political ideology that advocates state ownership of the means of production, the collectivization of labor, and the abolition of social class. It was the ideology of the Soviet Union (1917–89) and stood in contrast to free-market capitalism during the Cold War.

Cuban Missile Crisis (1962): the closest the United States and Soviet Union came to a nuclear exchange. It arose over a dispute between the US and USSR about deployment of Soviet missiles in Cuba.

Declinism: a belief that one's country or institution faces irreversible worsening in its overall position in the world.

Dynasty: a family line of heads of states.

The Economist: an English-language magazine, published in London since 1843, that analyzes economic and political issues at a relatively sophisticated level. Its editorial stance is "classical liberalism," which entails free enterprise and personal liberty.

European Economic Community (1958–93): an institution to support economic cooperation and coordination in Europe. The Maastricht Treaty of 1993 replaced it with the European Union.

European Union: founded in 1993 as a set of supranational (meaning above governments) and intergovernmental (meaning between governments) institutions. The EU administers and coordinates policy among 28 European states.

Falklands War (1982): a conflict between Argentina and the United Kingdom over the territory of the Falkland Islands in the South Atlantic. The conflict claimed nearly 1,000 lives and resulted in a British victory.

Financial crisis (2007–arguably ongoing): a major economic depression, the worst since the 1930s. Unemployment increased around the world, while economic production decreased.

Financial Times: an English-language newspaper, published in London beginning in 1888, which focuses on business and economics.

Foreign Affairs: a professional and academic journal founded in 1921. Published by the Council on Foreign Relations in New York, it offers an American focus on international politics.

Gross National Product (GNP): the market value of all goods and services produced in one year by the residents of a country.

Habsburg dynasty (1438–1918): a European family that, at its most powerful, ruled portions of southern Italy, Spain, Austria, the German city states, Hungary, and other areas in Central and Western Europe. It was known for using marriage rather than conquest to increase its political influence.

Hegemony: a concept relating to the dominance of a group by one individual—the "hegemon" is notable not only for compelling others to do or not do a thing, but for actually establishing the "rules of the game."

Hindenburg Programme (1916): the policy Germany adopted to vastly increase its military production in World War I. Ultimately, the plan (which diverted all German economic efforts to "war relevant" industries) led to disaster and starvation, and Germany's downfall.

Holy Roman Empire: a network of territories in Europe that endured from the ninth century until it was dissolved in 1806. The empire encompassed large parts of Austria, the Netherlands, Naples, and other territories around Europe.

International relations: the study of the relationships between states in a global system, primarily linked to foreign policy. It includes the study of supranational organizations such as the World Bank and other non-government organizations (NGOs).

Iraq War (2003–11): an armed conflict initially between Iraq and the United States, and then between a protracted insurgency and the United States. The United States and its allies believed that Saddam Hussein, the then-leader of Iraq, had secretly built a stockpile of nuclear weapons.

Korean War (1950–53): a war between North and South Korea, which arose from the division of Korea after World War II, and the tensions of the Cold War. A United Nations force led by the United States fought for the South; China fought for the North, with the help of the Soviet Union.

Longue durée: a French phrase meaning "long term." It refers, in the context of history, to the approach taken by the historians of the *Annales* school, who were concerned with historical changes (often social changes) over the long term.

Ming dynasty (1368–1644): a Chinese imperial dynasty. Ming rulers led a campaign to centralize Chinese institutions and created a standing army. They were also known for (partly) overseeing the building of grand structures such as the Great Wall.

Mongol Empire (1206–1368): the lands in Eurasia conquered by Mongolian warlord Temujin—better known as Genghis Khan—and his successors. At its peak it encompassed 1.27 million square miles from southeast Asia to eastern Europe.

Multipolar: an international order characterized by the equal importance of several state powers.

NATO: North Atlantic Treaty Organization, a military alliance between governments whose members guarantee to defend one another in the face of external attack. The alliance is led by the United States and has 28 members including all the major European powers. It derives from the North Atlantic Treaty, signed in the aftermath of World War II in 1949 by the US, France, Britain, Canada, and others.

Newcastle University: a public research university in Newcastle, founded in 1963.

9/11: a term referring to four coordinated terror attacks launched against the United States by the Islamic extremist group al-Qaeda on September 11, 2001. Four passenger airplanes were flown into various targets around the country, including the twin towers of the World Trade Center in New York City, and the Pentagon in Washington, DC.

Paradigm: a worldview that underpins the theories of a particular subject. For instance, the idea that states conflict, rather than cooperate, remains central to the paradigm of international relations realism.

Pax Americana: a Latin phrase meaning "American Peace." It refers to the long period of global stability (between great powers, if not domestically) in the second half of the twentieth century. But numerous proxy wars between the great powers, regimes throughout the global south sustained by authoritarian violence, and civil wars cast doubt on the overall peacefulness of the time.

Pax Britannica: a period of relative stability (at least between Western powers) experienced while Britain was at the height of its global power in the nineteenth century.

Polarity: the distribution of power within the international system—a bipolar system has power concentrated in two states, while a multipolar system has power concentrated in multiple states.

Reagan doctrine: a foreign policy strategy followed during the presidency of Ronald Reagan with the intention of diminishing the influence or power of the Soviet Union; anti-communist paramilitary forces were funded with the intention of destabilizing communist nations, and large sums of money were spent on arms provision.

Reserve currency: a stock of money held by governments so they may conduct international transactions. The US dollar is currently the most important currency, as it is the currency in which trades are agreed between states that do not use the US dollar as their native currency.

Roman Empire (27 B.C.E.–385 C.E.): the territorial holdings of the Roman state. The Roman Republic became the Empire when Julius Caesar declared himself dictator. At its height, it encompassed the entire Mediterranean, and significant portions of the Near East. In 385 C.E. it split into a western half, which fell to northern invasion in 476, and an eastern half, which became the Byzantine Empire, and fell to the Ottomans in 1453.

St. Antony's College: a postgraduate-only college at the University of Oxford, founded in 1950. It specializes in "area studies," meaning close study of a given geographic area, such as East Asia or Africa.

Socialism: a political system in which the means of production (the tools and resources required by business and industry) are held in common ownership.

Soft power: a concept developed by American political thinker Joseph Nye, Jr., the phrase refers to a form of cultural imperialism, leadership imposed through the "soft power" of US preeminence in technology, culture, or international governance through organizations such as the United Nations rather than the "hard power" associated with economic or military force.

South Korea: the southern half of the Korean peninsula in East Asia, South Korea has a highly advanced economy. Along with Hong Kong, Singapore and Taiwan (the "Asian Tigers"), it experienced rapid economic growth from the 1960s onward.

Soviet Union/Union of Soviet Socialist Republics (USSR): a super-state encompassing communist countries in Europe and Central Asia, with its capital in Moscow. Founded in 1922, it dissolved with the end of the Cold War in 1991.

Sphere of influence: a concept in politics, most significant during the Cold War. A state's "sphere of influence" represents an area in which they wield special authority, even over other states.

Superpower: a term most commonly used with reference to the United States and the Soviet Union in the Cold War, because these nations held more power than any other nation in history.

Taiwan: an island in East Asia, 180km (112 miles) off the coast of China, to the southeast. The country experienced rapid industrialization and economic growth toward the end of the twentieth century and, with South Korea, Hong Kong, and Singapore, is considered one of the "Asian Tigers."

Totalitarian: refers to a system of government in which obedience to the state remains the most important aspect of daily life.

United Nations: an intergovernmental organization representing (nearly) every state in the world. It is the main organization administering international health, development, security, and similar programs.

University of Oxford: a collegiate research-focused university in Oxford, in the United Kingdom. It is the oldest university in the English-speaking world. Teaching in Oxford began—it is believed—in the eleventh century, though the first of its colleges was founded in the thirteenth century; different colleges dispute this honor.

Vietnam War: a two-decade-long military conflict between communist forces, led by North Vietnam, and anti-communist forces, led by the United States and South Vietnam. Starting in 1955 and finishing in 1975 after American troops withdrew from Vietnamese territory, it was the longest proxy war fought by the United States during the Cold War.

Wall Street Journal: an English-language newspaper, published in New York since 1889, that focuses on business issues and economics.

War on Terror: the term commonly applied to American-led actions throughout the Middle East against non-state "terrorist" actors, including al-Qaeda. The effort includes the drone campaign in Pakistan, the occupation of Afghanistan, and other covert and overt operations.

Warsaw Pact (1955–91): a military alliance between the eight communist states in Eastern Europe that provided security guarantees to its members. The pact dissolved as the Cold War ended.

Weltpolitik: a German term meaning "world policy," and referring to a late-nineteenth-century German governmental policy that aimed to build up German military power while fostering an intense national pride and using tough diplomacy to establish Germany as a "great power."

World systems analysis: a method for analyzing global history that sees the "world system" of interconnecting capital and labor and other forces as the principal actor in historical change rather than "nation-states."

World War I: an international conflict from 1914 to 1918 centered in Europe and involving the major economic world powers of the day. The industrial advancements in military technology as well as the scale of the conflict resulted in vast military and civilian casualties. Some scholars see World War II as a continuation of World War I, because of unresolved tensions.

World War II: a global conflict from 1939 to 1945 that involved the world's great powers and numerous other countries around the globe. Fought between the Allies (the United States, Britain, France, the Soviet Union, and others) and the Axis powers (Germany, Italy, Japan, and others), it was seen as a major moral struggle between freedom and tyranny and included events like the Holocaust.

Yale University: an Ivy League university in the United States. Founded in 1701, it is the third oldest university in that country.

PEOPLE MENTIONED IN THE TEXT

Giovanni Arrighi (1937–2009) was an Italian political economist and historian. His work examined the evolution of international capitalism and its attendant ideas since 1400. A political activist as well as an academic, he was jailed in 1966 while teaching in Rhodesia (now Zimbabwe).

Otto von Bismarck (1815–98) was a nineteenth-century Prussian statesman. He is considered to have been the founder of modern Germany, and was the first chancellor of a united Germany.

Jeremy Black (born 1955) is a prolific British historian, professor of history at Exeter University in southwest England. He is a particular expert in eighteenth-century international relations and British politics.

Philip Bobbitt (b. 1948) is an American lawyer and civil servant, and an academic in the field of security studies. He has served under both Democratic and Republican governments, advising US presidents on intelligence, international law, and strategy.

Fernand Braudel (1902–85) was a French historian. Founder of the *Annales* school, he emphasized the role of large-scale, long-term socioeconomic shifts (rather than the decisions of kings) in driving history.

John Brewer is a historian at the University of California, Los Angeles, specializing in the seventeenth and eighteenth centuries.

Stephen Brooks is a professor of government at Dartmouth University. He is a public intellectual advocating a "forward" American policy. "Forward" means being open to commitments abroad, and seeking an active role in solving global problems (economically, militarily, and so forth). This policy is about increasing influence rather than conserving resources.

Charles V (1500–58) was king of Spain (as Carlos I), and was also elected Holy Roman Emperor (the elected ruler of a confederation of semi-independent princely states in an area that comprises much of central Europe) in 1519. His reign was characterized by imperial expansion in the New World, and war against the French in Europe.

Christopher Columbus (1451–1506) was an Italian explorer. Though he was looking for an alternative route to India, Columbus sailed from Europe across the Atlantic to America in 1492.

John Crace is a British journalist and author who writes in the *Guardian*. He currently writes a regular sketch on events in the House of Commons in the British Parliament.

Dr. Faustus is a character in Germanic folklore, made famous in the English language in a play by the English playwright Christopher Marlowe, first performed in 1592. He famously made a bargain with the devil, trading his immortal soul for knowledge.

Niall Ferguson (b. 1964) is a Scottish historian and popular writer, who often focuses on the special role of the West and capitalism in world history. He is occasionally the subject of media controversy due to remarks on Islam or colonialism.

John Lewis Gaddis (b. 1941) is an American professor of military and naval history at Yale University. He is considered to be the most important Cold War historian. His approach (the "great man theory") has been characterized as highlighting the role played by individuals.

John Andrew Gallagher (1919–80) was a British historian of empire at the universities of Oxford and Cambridge. His (co-written) article, "The Imperialism of Free Trade," has been called the most-cited article ever published in the discipline of history.

Samuel Huntington (1927–2008) was an American political theorist. His 1993 article "The Clash of Civilizations?" (later developed into a book) earned him fame and notoriety. It argued that in the post-Cold War era, international conflicts would be defined by cultural divisions.

John Ikenberry (b. 1954) is an American theorist of international relations at Princeton University. He is, famously, one of the architects of the US policy of "liberal internationalism."

Charles Krauthammer (b. 1950) is an American public intellectual and Pulitzer Prize-winning journalist. He advocates a tough but restrained American foreign policy. He originated the phrase "Reagan doctrine."

Charles Kupchan (b. 1958) is an American academic, professor of international affairs at Georgetown University and a senior fellow at the Council of Foreign Relations. Kupchan focuses on the possibility of peace and change in international affairs.

Christopher Layne (b. 1949) is the chair of intelligence and national security at Texas A&M University. He is notable for critiquing the ambitions of liberal internationalists to spread American values abroad.

Richard Ned Lebow (b. 1942) is an American political scientist and professor of international political theory at King's College London. He is considered the founder of Neoclassical Realism, an approach that holds that personality and the balance of power both remain important in determining international outcomes.

Sir Basil Liddell Hart (1895–1970) was a British military theorist at the University of Oxford. He is credited with influencing the development of rapid, tank-based warfare in the aftermath of the stationary, trench-based strategy of World War I.

Edward Luttwak (b. 1942) is an American military and political theorist. He focuses on "grand" strategy, and has written about how it has manifested itself as far back as the Roman Empire.

William McNeill (b. 1917) is a Canadian American professor (emeritus) of history at the University of Chicago. He won the National Humanities Medal in the US in 2010, recognizing his contribution to history and his teaching work.

Henry Nau (b. 1941) is professor of political science and international affairs at George Washington University. He sat on the National Security Council during the Reagan administration.

Joseph Nye, Jr. (b. 1937) is an American political science professor at Harvard University. He co-wrote *Power and Interdependence* with the American academic Robert Keohane, effectively helping found neoliberalism. He is also considered to be the father of theories of "complex interdependence," which illustrate how states will avoid conflict with other states when their interests are bound up with each other's success.

Richard Perle (b. 1941) is an American political consultant and former member of the Senate Armed Services Committee who also served as assistant secretary of defense under President Reagan. Today a member of many think tanks, he is a prominent member of a group of neoconservatives ("neo-cons") seeking to influence US foreign policy.

Philip II (1527–98): king of Spain, who also ruled swathes of territory throughout Europe (including, briefly, England and Ireland by virtue of his marriage to Mary I of England). During his period of influence, Spain conquered territory around the world, including the Philippines (which was named after him).

Barry Posen (b. 1962) is professor of political science at the Massachusetts Institute of Technology (MIT). He is famous for his focus on the interaction between military doctrine and foreign policy.

Leopold von Ranke (1795–1886) was a German historian, and pioneered the use of rigorous sources in the study of history. Von Ranke's rigorous approach to history has been influential.

Ronald Reagan (1911–2004) was 40th president of the United States (1981–89). A member of the Republican Party, he is widely credited in the United States with having won the Cold War. He is also remembered for promoting nationalism and the global free market.

J. L. Richardson is a lecturer in government at the University of Sydney.

Friedrich Schiller (1759–1805) was a German polymath (someone with wide knowledge in many fields). He was one of the early historians of the Thirty Years' War, but is best known as a literary figure.

Oswald Spengler (1880–1936) was a German historian (among other things), most famous for postulating that civilizations are akin to organisms with lifespans.

Joseph Stalin (1878–1953) was leader of the Soviet Union as General Secretary of the Communist Party from 1922 to his death. His brutal economic policies and political repression caused the deaths of millions, but also made the Soviet Union into a superpower. His successor, Nikita Khruschev, denounced him as a tyrant.

Janice Gross Stein (b. 1943) is a Canadian political scientist at the Munk School of Global Affairs at the University of Toronto. She writes on many topics, including diplomacy, negotiation, and intelligence.

A. J. P. Taylor (1906–90) was a British historian who wrote on nineteenth- and twentieth-century political and diplomatic history. He is the author of the classic *The Origins of the Second World War* (1961).

Harry S. Truman (1884–1972) was the 33rd president of the United States (1945–53). He presided over the beginning of the Cold War and helped pioneer the "containment" strategy (the Truman doctrine) of keeping the Soviets from gaining international influence.

Immanuel Wallerstein (b. 1930) is an American sociologist and international historian. He is famous for his theory of the "world system," which argues that unequal economic exchange between a set of privileged "core" states (including the United States and Europe) and unprivileged "peripheral" states (such as Africa, South America, and South Asia) characterizes modern international politics.

Kenneth Waltz (1924–2013) was an American international relations professor best known for reformulating realism to make it more scientific (this is often called neorealism). Neorealism argued that states are naturally suspicious of one another and prone to secure their position by balancing power. This theory dominated international relations from the 1970s to the 1990s.

William Wohlforth (b. 1959) is professor of government at Dartmouth College. His work emphasizes security and foreign policy.

Fareed Zakaria (b. 1964) is an Indian American journalist and author. He has been managing editor of *Foreign Affairs* and *Time*, and notably wrote *The Post-American World*. He believes the United States' importance has declined, but that it is in no danger from countries that consider the United States increasingly irrelevant.

WORKS CITED

WORKS CITED

Acherson, Neal. "Interview with Paul Kennedy." *Independent*, March 28, 1993. Accessed September 12, 2015. http://www.independent.co.uk/voices/interview--prepare-to-meet-thy-future-big-books-about-the-21st-century-are-supposed-to-make-your-flesh-creep-but-paul-kennedy-argues-that-the-end-of-the-world-is-not-quite-nigh-1500508.html.

Arrighi, Giovanni. *The Long Twentieth Century: Money, Power, and the Origins of Our Times.* London: Verso, 2002.

Black, Jeremy. *Great Powers and the Quest for Hegemony: The World Order Since 1500.* London: Routledge, 2008.

Bobbitt, Philip. *The Shield of Achilles: War, Peace and Course of History.* London: Allen Lane, 2002.

_____. *Terror and Consent: The Wars for the Twenty-first Century.* London: Allen Lane, 2008.

Braudel, Fernand. *The Mediterranean and Mediterranean World in the Age of Philip II.* Translated by Siân Reynolds. New York: Harper & Row, 1972.

Brewer, John. *The Sinews of Power: War, Money, and the English State 1688–1783.* London: Century Hutchinson, 1988.

Brooks, Stephen, John Ikenberry, and William Wohlforth. "Lean Forward: In Defense of American Engagement." *Foreign Affairs* 92, no. 1 (2013): 130–42.

Chua, Amy. *Day of Empire: How Hyperpowers Rise to Global Dominance—And Why They Fall.* London: Doubleday, 2007.

Clark, William P. *United States National Security Decision Directive 75.* Washington, DC: 1983.

Crace, John. "Paul Kennedy: Neocons' worst nightmare." *Guardian*, February 5, 2008. Accessed September 3, 2015. http://www.theguardian.com/education/2008/feb/05/academicexperts.highereducationprofile.

Craig, Gordon A. "The Historian and the Study of International Relations." *American Historical Review* 88, no. 1 (1983): 1–11.

Epstein, Katherine. "Scholarship and the Ship of State: Rethinking the Anglo-American Strategic Decline Analogy." *International Affairs* 91, issue 2 (2015): 319–31.

Ferguson, Niall. *Civilization: The West and the Rest.* London: Allen Lane, 2010.

Finney, Patrick. "Introduction: What is International History?" in *Palgrave Advances in International History*, edited by Patrick Finney, 1–36. Basingstoke: Palgrave Macmillan, 2005.

Fukuyama, Francis. *The End of History and the Last Man*. New York: Free Press, 2006.

Gaddis, John Lewis. "The Long Peace: Elements of Stability in the Postwar International System." *International Security* 10, no. 4 (1986): 99–142.

_____. "International Relations Theory and the End of the Cold War." *International Security* 17, no. 3 (1992): 5–58.

Garthoff, Raymond L. *The Great Transition: American–Soviet Relations and the End of the Cold War.* Washington, DC: Brookings Institution, 1994.

Herodotus, *Histories*. Translated by A. M. Bowie. Cambridge: Cambridge University Press, 2007.

Huntington, Samuel. "The US: Decline or Renewal?" *Foreign Affairs* 67, no. 2 (1988): 76–96.

Ikenberry, John. "Imperial Overstretch?" *The Economist*, June 27, 2002. Accessed September 12, 2015. http://www.economist.com/node/1188741.

_____. "Review of *Parliament of Man*." *Foreign Affairs* 85, no. 6 (2006): 156.

Kennedy, Paul. *The Rise and Fall of British Naval Mastery.* London: Allen Lane, 1976.

_____. *The Rise of the Anglo-German Antagonism: 1860–1914*. London: George Allen & Unwin, 1980.

_____. *The Rise and Fall of the Great Powers*. New York: Vintage Books, 1989.

_____. *Preparing for the 21st Century*. New York: Random House, 1993.

_____. "The Eagle Has Landed." *Financial Times*, February 1, 2002.

_____. *The Parliament of Man: The Past, Present, and Future of the United Nations*. New York: Random House, 2006.

_____. "The Distant Horizon: What Can 'Big History' Tell Us About America's Future?" *Foreign Affairs* 87, no. 3 (2008): 126–32.

_____. "The Imperial Mind: A Historian's Education in the Ways of Empire." *The Atlantic*, January 2008. Accessed September 3, 2015. http://www.theatlantic.com/magazine/archive/2008/01/the-imperial-mind/306566/.

_____. "American Power is on the Wane." *Wall Street Journal*, January 1, 2009. Accessed September 14, 2015. http://www.wsj.com/articles/SB123189377673479433.

_____. "Asia's Rise: Rise and Fall." *The World Today* 66, no. 8/9 (2010): 6–9.

Kennedy, Paul, and Edward Luttwak. "*The Rise and Fall of the Great Powers*: An Exchange." *American Scholar* 59, no. 2 (1990): 283–9.

Kennedy, Paul, Richard Perle, and Joseph Nye, Jr. "The Reluctant Empire: In a Time of Great Consequence." *Brown Journal of World Affairs* 10, no. 1 (2003): 11–31.

Knutsen, Tobjorn. *History of International Relations Theory.* Manchester: Manchester University Press, 1997.

Krauthammer, Charles. "The Unipolar Moment." *Foreign Affairs* 70, no. 1 (1990/91): 23–33.

Kupchan, Charles. "Empire, Military Power, and Economic Decline." *International Security* 13, no. 4 (1989): 36–53.

LaFeber, Walter. *America, Russia, and the Cold War, 1945–2002*. New York: McGraw Hill, 2002.

von Laue, Theodore H. *Leopold Ranke: The Formative Years*. Princeton, NJ: Princeton University Press, 1950.

Layne, Christopher. "The End of the Pax Americana: How Western Decline Became Inevitable." *The Atlantic*, April 2012. Accessed September 14, 2015. http://www.theatlantic.com/international/archive/2012/04/the-end-of-pax-americana-how-western-decline-became-inevitable/256388/.

Lebow, Richard Ned, and Janice Gross Stein. "Reagan and the Russians." *Atlantic Monthly*, February 1994. Accessed September 12, 2015. http://www.theatlantic.com/past/politics/foreign/reagrus.htm.

Lieberthal, Kenneth, and Wang Jisi. *Addressing US–China Strategic Distrust*. Washington, DC: Brookings Institution, 2012.

McNeill, William. "*The Rise of the West* After Twenty-five Years," *Journal of World History* 1, no. 1 (1990): 1–21.

_____. *The Rise of the West: A History of the Human Community*. Chicago: University of Chicago Press, 1991.

Nau, Henry. "Why *The Rise and Fall of the Great Powers* Was Wrong." *Review of International Studies* 27, no. 4 (2001): 579–92.

Nye, Jr., Joseph. "The Changing Nature of World Power." *Political Science Quarterly* 105, issue 2 (1990) 2: 177–92.

_____. "Soft Power," *Foreign Policy* no. 80 (1990): 153–71.

Posen, Barry. "Pull Back: The Case for a Less Activist Foreign Policy." *Foreign Affairs* 92, no. 1 (2013): 116–28.

von Ranke, Leopold. *History of the Latin and Teutonic Peoples 1494–1514*. Translated by G. R. Dennis. London: George Bell and Sons, 1909.

Richards, Huw. "Redrawing the Big Picture." *Times Higher Education*, August 28, 2008. Accessed September 2, 2015, https://www.timeshighereducation.co.uk/features/redrawing-the-big-picture/403290.article.

Richardson, J. L. "Paul Kennedy and International Relations Theory: A Comparison with Robert Gilpin." *Australian Journal of International Affairs* 45, no. 1 (1991): 70–7.

Roberts, M. "The Military Revolution, 1560–1600." In *Essays in Swedish History*, edited by M. Roberts, 195–226. London: Weidenfeld & Nicolson, 1967.

Robinson, Ronald, John Gallagher, and Alice Denny. *Africa and the Victorians: The Official Mind of Imperialism*. Basingstoke: Macmillan, 1981.

Rostow, W. W. "Beware of Historians Bearing False Analogies." *Foreign Affairs* 66, no. 4 (1988): 863–8.

Schulin, Ernst. "Ranke's Universal History and National History." *Syracuse Scholar* 9, issue 1 (1988): 1–8.

Spengler, Oswald. *The Decline of the West*. Edited by Helmut Werner. Translated by Charles F. Atkinson. Oxford: Oxford University Press, 1991.

Taylor, A. J. P. *The Struggle for Mastery in Europe 1848–1918*. Oxford: Oxford University Press, 1969.

Thucydides. *History of the Peloponnesian War*. Edited and translated by Jeremy Mynott. Cambridge: Cambridge University Press, 2013.

Toynbee, Arnold. *A Study of History: Abridgement of Volumes I–VI*. Edited by D. C. Somervell. Oxford: Oxford University Press, 1987.

Wallerstein, Immanuel. *The Modern World System I: Capitalist Agriculture and the Origins of the European World-Economy in the Sixteenth Century, with a New Prologue*. Berkeley: University of California Press, 2011.

Waltz, Kenneth. *Theory of International Politics*. Reading: Addison Wesley, 1979.

Zakaria, Fareed. *The Post-American World*. New York: W. W. Norton and Company, 2008.

THE MACAT LIBRARY
BY DISCIPLINE

AFRICANA STUDIES

Chinua Achebe's *An Image of Africa: Racism in Conrad's Heart of Darkness*
W. E. B. Du Bois's *The Souls of Black Folk*
Zora Neale Huston's *Characteristics of Negro Expression*
Martin Luther King Jr's *Why We Can't Wait*
Toni Morrison's *Playing in the Dark: Whiteness in the American Literary Imagination*

ANTHROPOLOGY

Arjun Appadurai's *Modernity at Large: Cultural Dimensions of Globalisation*
Philippe Ariès's *Centuries of Childhood*
Franz Boas's *Race, Language and Culture*
Kim Chan & Renée Mauborgne's *Blue Ocean Strategy*
Jared Diamond's *Guns, Germs & Steel: the Fate of Human Societies*
Jared Diamond's *Collapse: How Societies Choose to Fail or Survive*
E. E. Evans-Pritchard's *Witchcraft, Oracles and Magic Among the Azande*
James Ferguson's *The Anti-Politics Machine*
Clifford Geertz's *The Interpretation of Cultures*
David Graeber's *Debt: the First 5000 Years*
Karen Ho's *Liquidated: An Ethnography of Wall Street*
Geert Hofstede's *Culture's Consequences: Comparing Values, Behaviors, Institutes and Organizations across Nations*
Claude Lévi-Strauss's *Structural Anthropology*
Jay Macleod's *Ain't No Makin' It: Aspirations and Attainment in a Low-Income Neighborhood*
Saba Mahmood's *The Politics of Piety: The Islamic Revival and the Feminist Subject*
Marcel Mauss's *The Gift*

BUSINESS

Jean Lave & Etienne Wenger's *Situated Learning*
Theodore Levitt's *Marketing Myopia*
Burton G. Malkiel's *A Random Walk Down Wall Street*
Douglas McGregor's *The Human Side of Enterprise*
Michael Porter's *Competitive Strategy: Creating and Sustaining Superior Performance*
John Kotter's *Leading Change*
C. K. Prahalad & Gary Hamel's *The Core Competence of the Corporation*

CRIMINOLOGY

Michelle Alexander's *The New Jim Crow: Mass Incarceration in the Age of Colorblindness*
Michael R. Gottfredson & Travis Hirschi's *A General Theory of Crime*
Richard Herrnstein & Charles A. Murray's *The Bell Curve: Intelligence and Class Structure in American Life*
Elizabeth Loftus's *Eyewitness Testimony*
Jay Macleod's *Ain't No Makin' It: Aspirations and Attainment in a Low-Income Neighborhood*
Philip Zimbardo's *The Lucifer Effect*

ECONOMICS

Janet Abu-Lughod's *Before European Hegemony*
Ha-Joon Chang's *Kicking Away the Ladder*
David Brion Davis's *The Problem of Slavery in the Age of Revolution*
Milton Friedman's *The Role of Monetary Policy*
Milton Friedman's *Capitalism and Freedom*
David Graeber's *Debt: the First 5000 Years*
Friedrich Hayek's *The Road to Serfdom*
Karen Ho's *Liquidated: An Ethnography of Wall Street*

The Macat Library By Discipline

John Maynard Keynes's *The General Theory of Employment, Interest and Money*
Charles P. Kindleberger's *Manias, Panics and Crashes*
Robert Lucas's *Why Doesn't Capital Flow from Rich to Poor Countries?*
Burton G. Malkiel's *A Random Walk Down Wall Street*
Thomas Robert Malthus's *An Essay on the Principle of Population*
Karl Marx's *Capital*
Thomas Piketty's *Capital in the Twenty-First Century*
Amartya Sen's *Development as Freedom*
Adam Smith's *The Wealth of Nations*
Nassim Nicholas Taleb's *The Black Swan: The Impact of the Highly Improbable*
Amos Tversky's & Daniel Kahneman's *Judgment under Uncertainty: Heuristics and Biases*
Mahbub Ul Haq's *Reflections on Human Development*
Max Weber's *The Protestant Ethic and the Spirit of Capitalism*

FEMINISM AND GENDER STUDIES

Judith Butler's *Gender Trouble*
Simone De Beauvoir's *The Second Sex*
Michel Foucault's *History of Sexuality*
Betty Friedan's *The Feminine Mystique*
Saba Mahmood's *The Politics of Piety: The Islamic Revival and the Feminist Subject*
Joan Wallach Scott's *Gender and the Politics of History*
Mary Wollstonecraft's *A Vindication of the Rights of Woman*
Virginia Woolf's *A Room of One's Own*

GEOGRAPHY

The Brundtland Report's *Our Common Future*
Rachel Carson's *Silent Spring*
Charles Darwin's *On the Origin of Species*
James Ferguson's *The Anti-Politics Machine*
Jane Jacobs's *The Death and Life of Great American Cities*
James Lovelock's *Gaia: A New Look at Life on Earth*
Amartya Sen's *Development as Freedom*
Mathis Wackernagel & William Rees's *Our Ecological Footprint*

HISTORY

Janet Abu-Lughod's *Before European Hegemony*
Benedict Anderson's *Imagined Communities*
Bernard Bailyn's *The Ideological Origins of the American Revolution*
Hanna Batatu's *The Old Social Classes And The Revolutionary Movements Of Iraq*
Christopher Browning's *Ordinary Men: Reserve Police Batallion 101 and the Final Solution in Poland*
Edmund Burke's *Reflections on the Revolution in France*
William Cronon's *Nature's Metropolis: Chicago And The Great West*
Alfred W. Crosby's *The Columbian Exchange*
Hamid Dabashi's *Iran: A People Interrupted*
David Brion Davis's *The Problem of Slavery in the Age of Revolution*
Nathalie Zemon Davis's *The Return of Martin Guerre*
Jared Diamond's *Guns, Germs & Steel: the Fate of Human Societies*
Frank Dikotter's *Mao's Great Famine*
John W Dower's *War Without Mercy: Race And Power In The Pacific War*
W. E. B. Du Bois's *The Souls of Black Folk*
Richard J. Evans's *In Defence of History*
Lucien Febvre's *The Problem of Unbelief in the 16th Century*
Sheila Fitzpatrick's *Everyday Stalinism*

Eric Foner's *Reconstruction: America's Unfinished Revolution, 1863-1877*
Michel Foucault's *Discipline and Punish*
Michel Foucault's *History of Sexuality*
Francis Fukuyama's *The End of History and the Last Man*
John Lewis Gaddis's *We Now Know: Rethinking Cold War History*
Ernest Gellner's *Nations and Nationalism*
Eugene Genovese's *Roll, Jordan, Roll: The World the Slaves Made*
Carlo Ginzburg's *The Night Battles*
Daniel Goldhagen's *Hitler's Willing Executioners*
Jack Goldstone's *Revolution and Rebellion in the Early Modern World*
Antonio Gramsci's *The Prison Notebooks*
Alexander Hamilton, John Jay & James Madison's *The Federalist Papers*
Christopher Hill's *The World Turned Upside Down*
Carole Hillenbrand's *The Crusades: Islamic Perspectives*
Thomas Hobbes's *Leviathan*
Eric Hobsbawm's *The Age Of Revolution*
John A. Hobson's *Imperialism: A Study*
Albert Hourani's *History of the Arab Peoples*
Samuel P. Huntington's *The Clash of Civilizations and the Remaking of World Order*
C. L. R. James's *The Black Jacobins*
Tony Judt's *Postwar: A History of Europe Since 1945*
Ernst Kantorowicz's *The King's Two Bodies: A Study in Medieval Political Theology*
Paul Kennedy's *The Rise and Fall of the Great Powers*
Ian Kershaw's *The "Hitler Myth": Image and Reality in the Third Reich*
John Maynard Keynes's *The General Theory of Employment, Interest and Money*
Charles P. Kindleberger's *Manias, Panics and Crashes*
Martin Luther King Jr's *Why We Can't Wait*
Henry Kissinger's *World Order: Reflections on the Character of Nations and the Course of History*
Thomas Kuhn's *The Structure of Scientific Revolutions*
Georges Lefebvre's *The Coming of the French Revolution*
John Locke's *Two Treatises of Government*
Niccolò Machiavelli's *The Prince*
Thomas Robert Malthus's *An Essay on the Principle of Population*
Mahmood Mamdani's *Citizen and Subject: Contemporary Africa And The Legacy Of Late Colonialism*
Karl Marx's *Capital*
Stanley Milgram's *Obedience to Authority*
John Stuart Mill's *On Liberty*
Thomas Paine's *Common Sense*
Thomas Paine's *Rights of Man*
Geoffrey Parker's *Global Crisis: War, Climate Change and Catastrophe in the Seventeenth Century*
Jonathan Riley-Smith's *The First Crusade and the Idea of Crusading*
Jean-Jacques Rousseau's *The Social Contract*
Joan Wallach Scott's *Gender and the Politics of History*
Theda Skocpol's *States and Social Revolutions*
Adam Smith's *The Wealth of Nations*
Timothy Snyder's *Bloodlands: Europe Between Hitler and Stalin*
Sun Tzu's *The Art of War*
Keith Thomas's *Religion and the Decline of Magic*
Thucydides's *The History of the Peloponnesian War*
Frederick Jackson Turner's *The Significance of the Frontier in American History*
Odd Arne Westad's *The Global Cold War: Third World Interventions And The Making Of Our Times*

LITERATURE

Chinua Achebe's *An Image of Africa: Racism in Conrad's Heart of Darkness*
Roland Barthes's *Mythologies*
Homi K. Bhabha's *The Location of Culture*
Judith Butler's *Gender Trouble*
Simone De Beauvoir's *The Second Sex*
Ferdinand De Saussure's *Course in General Linguistics*
T. S. Eliot's *The Sacred Wood: Essays on Poetry and Criticism*
Zora Neale Huston's *Characteristics of Negro Expression*
Toni Morrison's *Playing in the Dark: Whiteness in the American Literary Imagination*
Edward Said's *Orientalism*
Gayatri Chakravorty Spivak's *Can the Subaltern Speak?*
Mary Wollstonecraft's *A Vindication of the Rights of Women*
Virginia Woolf's *A Room of One's Own*

PHILOSOPHY

Elizabeth Anscombe's *Modern Moral Philosophy*
Hannah Arendt's *The Human Condition*
Aristotle's *Metaphysics*
Aristotle's *Nicomachean Ethics*
Edmund Gettier's *Is Justified True Belief Knowledge?*
Georg Wilhelm Friedrich Hegel's *Phenomenology of Spirit*
David Hume's *Dialogues Concerning Natural Religion*
David Hume's *The Enquiry for Human Understanding*
Immanuel Kant's *Religion within the Boundaries of Mere Reason*
Immanuel Kant's *Critique of Pure Reason*
Søren Kierkegaard's *The Sickness Unto Death*
Søren Kierkegaard's *Fear and Trembling*
C. S. Lewis's *The Abolition of Man*
Alasdair MacIntyre's *After Virtue*
Marcus Aurelius's *Meditations*
Friedrich Nietzsche's *On the Genealogy of Morality*
Friedrich Nietzsche's *Beyond Good and Evil*
Plato's *Republic*
Plato's *Symposium*
Jean-Jacques Rousseau's *The Social Contract*
Gilbert Ryle's *The Concept of Mind*
Baruch Spinoza's *Ethics*
Sun Tzu's *The Art of War*
Ludwig Wittgenstein's *Philosophical Investigations*

POLITICS

Benedict Anderson's *Imagined Communities*
Aristotle's *Politics*
Bernard Bailyn's *The Ideological Origins of the American Revolution*
Edmund Burke's *Reflections on the Revolution in France*
John C. Calhoun's *A Disquisition on Government*
Ha-Joon Chang's *Kicking Away the Ladder*
Hamid Dabashi's *Iran: A People Interrupted*
Hamid Dabashi's *Theology of Discontent: The Ideological Foundation of the Islamic Revolution in Iran*
Robert Dahl's *Democracy and its Critics*
Robert Dahl's *Who Governs?*
David Brion Davis's *The Problem of Slavery in the Age of Revolution*

Alexis De Tocqueville's *Democracy in America*
James Ferguson's *The Anti-Politics Machine*
Frank Dikotter's *Mao's Great Famine*
Sheila Fitzpatrick's *Everyday Stalinism*
Eric Foner's *Reconstruction: America's Unfinished Revolution, 1863-1877*
Milton Friedman's *Capitalism and Freedom*
Francis Fukuyama's *The End of History and the Last Man*
John Lewis Gaddis's *We Now Know: Rethinking Cold War History*
Ernest Gellner's *Nations and Nationalism*
David Graeber's *Debt: the First 5000 Years*
Antonio Gramsci's *The Prison Notebooks*
Alexander Hamilton, John Jay & James Madison's *The Federalist Papers*
Friedrich Hayek's *The Road to Serfdom*
Christopher Hill's *The World Turned Upside Down*
Thomas Hobbes's *Leviathan*
John A. Hobson's *Imperialism: A Study*
Samuel P. Huntington's *The Clash of Civilizations and the Remaking of World Order*
Tony Judt's *Postwar: A History of Europe Since 1945*
David C. Kang's *China Rising: Peace, Power and Order in East Asia*
Paul Kennedy's *The Rise and Fall of Great Powers*
Robert Keohane's *After Hegemony*
Martin Luther King Jr.'s *Why We Can't Wait*
Henry Kissinger's *World Order: Reflections on the Character of Nations and the Course of History*
John Locke's *Two Treatises of Government*
Niccolò Machiavelli's *The Prince*
Thomas Robert Malthus's *An Essay on the Principle of Population*
Mahmood Mamdani's *Citizen and Subject: Contemporary Africa And The Legacy Of Late Colonialism*
Karl Marx's *Capital*
John Stuart Mill's *On Liberty*
John Stuart Mill's *Utilitarianism*
Hans Morgenthau's *Politics Among Nations*
Thomas Paine's *Common Sense*
Thomas Paine's *Rights of Man*
Thomas Piketty's *Capital in the Twenty-First Century*
Robert D. Putman's *Bowling Alone*
John Rawls's *Theory of Justice*
Jean-Jacques Rousseau's *The Social Contract*
Theda Skocpol's *States and Social Revolutions*
Adam Smith's *The Wealth of Nations*
Sun Tzu's *The Art of War*
Henry David Thoreau's *Civil Disobedience*
Thucydides's *The History of the Peloponnesian War*
Kenneth Waltz's *Theory of International Politics*
Max Weber's *Politics as a Vocation*
Odd Arne Westad's *The Global Cold War: Third World Interventions And The Making Of Our Times*

POSTCOLONIAL STUDIES

Roland Barthes's *Mythologies*
Frantz Fanon's *Black Skin, White Masks*
Homi K. Bhabha's *The Location of Culture*
Gustavo Gutiérrez's *A Theology of Liberation*
Edward Said's *Orientalism*
Gayatri Chakravorty Spivak's *Can the Subaltern Speak?*

PSYCHOLOGY

Gordon Allport's *The Nature of Prejudice*
Alan Baddeley & Graham Hitch's *Aggression: A Social Learning Analysis*
Albert Bandura's *Aggression: A Social Learning Analysis*
Leon Festinger's *A Theory of Cognitive Dissonance*
Sigmund Freud's *The Interpretation of Dreams*
Betty Friedan's *The Feminine Mystique*
Michael R. Gottfredson & Travis Hirschi's *A General Theory of Crime*
Eric Hoffer's *The True Believer: Thoughts on the Nature of Mass Movements*
William James's *Principles of Psychology*
Elizabeth Loftus's *Eyewitness Testimony*
A. H. Maslow's *A Theory of Human Motivation*
Stanley Milgram's *Obedience to Authority*
Steven Pinker's *The Better Angels of Our Nature*
Oliver Sacks's *The Man Who Mistook His Wife For a Hat*
Richard Thaler & Cass Sunstein's *Nudge: Improving Decisions About Health, Wealth and Happiness*
Amos Tversky's *Judgment under Uncertainty: Heuristics and Biases*
Philip Zimbardo's *The Lucifer Effect*

SCIENCE

Rachel Carson's *Silent Spring*
William Cronon's *Nature's Metropolis: Chicago And The Great West*
Alfred W. Crosby's *The Columbian Exchange*
Charles Darwin's *On the Origin of Species*
Richard Dawkin's *The Selfish Gene*
Thomas Kuhn's *The Structure of Scientific Revolutions*
Geoffrey Parker's *Global Crisis: War, Climate Change and Catastrophe in the Seventeenth Century*
Mathis Wackernagel & William Rees's *Our Ecological Footprint*

SOCIOLOGY

Michelle Alexander's *The New Jim Crow: Mass Incarceration in the Age of Colorblindness*
Gordon Allport's *The Nature of Prejudice*
Albert Bandura's *Aggression: A Social Learning Analysis*
Hanna Batatu's *The Old Social Classes And The Revolutionary Movements Of Iraq*
Ha-Joon Chang's *Kicking Away the Ladder*
W. E. B. Du Bois's *The Souls of Black Folk*
Émile Durkheim's *On Suicide*
Frantz Fanon's *Black Skin, White Masks*
Frantz Fanon's *The Wretched of the Earth*
Eric Foner's *Reconstruction: America's Unfinished Revolution, 1863-1877*
Eugene Genovese's *Roll, Jordan, Roll: The World the Slaves Made*
Jack Goldstone's *Revolution and Rebellion in the Early Modern World*
Antonio Gramsci's *The Prison Notebooks*
Richard Herrnstein & Charles A Murray's *The Bell Curve: Intelligence and Class Structure in American Life*
Eric Hoffer's *The True Believer: Thoughts on the Nature of Mass Movements*
Jane Jacobs's *The Death and Life of Great American Cities*
Robert Lucas's *Why Doesn't Capital Flow from Rich to Poor Countries?*
Jay Macleod's *Ain't No Makin' It: Aspirations and Attainment in a Low Income Neighborhood*
Elaine May's *Homeward Bound: American Families in the Cold War Era*
Douglas McGregor's *The Human Side of Enterprise*
C. Wright Mills's *The Sociological Imagination*

Thomas Piketty's *Capital in the Twenty-First Century*
Robert D. Putman's *Bowling Alone*
David Riesman's *The Lonely Crowd: A Study of the Changing American Character*
Edward Said's *Orientalism*
Joan Wallach Scott's *Gender and the Politics of History*
Theda Skocpol's *States and Social Revolutions*
Max Weber's *The Protestant Ethic and the Spirit of Capitalism*

THEOLOGY

Augustine's *Confessions*
Benedict's *Rule of St Benedict*
Gustavo Gutiérrez's *A Theology of Liberation*
Carole Hillenbrand's *The Crusades: Islamic Perspectives*
David Hume's *Dialogues Concerning Natural Religion*
Immanuel Kant's *Religion within the Boundaries of Mere Reason*
Ernst Kantorowicz's *The King's Two Bodies: A Study in Medieval Political Theology*
Søren Kierkegaard's *The Sickness Unto Death*
C. S. Lewis's *The Abolition of Man*
Saba Mahmood's *The Politics of Piety: The Islamic Revival and the Feminist Subject*
Baruch Spinoza's *Ethics*
Keith Thomas's *Religion and the Decline of Magic*

COMING SOON

Chris Argyris's *The Individual and the Organisation*
Seyla Benhabib's *The Rights of Others*
Walter Benjamin's *The Work Of Art in the Age of Mechanical Reproduction*
John Berger's *Ways of Seeing*
Pierre Bourdieu's *Outline of a Theory of Practice*
Mary Douglas's *Purity and Danger*
Roland Dworkin's *Taking Rights Seriously*
James G. March's *Exploration and Exploitation in Organisational Learning*
Ikujiro Nonaka's *A Dynamic Theory of Organizational Knowledge Creation*
Griselda Pollock's *Vision and Difference*
Amartya Sen's *Inequality Re-Examined*
Susan Sontag's *On Photography*
Yasser Tabbaa's *The Transformation of Islamic Art*
Ludwig von Mises's *Theory of Money and Credit*

Macat Disciplines

Access the greatest ideas and thinkers across entire disciplines, including

TOTALITARIANISM

Sheila Fitzpatrick's, *Everyday Stalinism*
Ian Kershaw's, *The "Hitler Myth"*
Timothy Snyder's, *Bloodlands*

Macat analyses are available from all good bookshops and libraries.

Access hundreds of analyses through one, multimedia tool.
Join free for one month **library.macat.com**

Macat Pairs

*Analyse historical and modern issues
from opposite sides of an argument.
Pairs include:*

RACE AND IDENTITY

Zora Neale Hurston's
Characteristics of Negro Expression
Using material collected on anthropological
expeditions to the South, Zora Neale Hurston explains
how expression in African American culture in the
early twentieth century departs from the art of white
America. At the time, African American art was often
criticized for copying white culture. For Hurston, this
criticism misunderstood how art works. European
tradition views art as something fixed. But Hurston
describes a creative process that is alive, ever-
changing, and largely improvisational. She maintains
that African American art works through a process
called 'mimicry'—where an imitated object or verbal
pattern, for example, is reshaped and altered until
it becomes something new, novel—and worthy of
attention.

Frantz Fanon's
Black Skin, White Masks
Black Skin, White Masks offers a radical analysis of the
psychological effects of colonization on the colonized.

Fanon witnessed the effects of colonization first
hand both in his birthplace, Martinique, and again
later in life when he worked as a psychiatrist
in another French colony, Algeria. His text is
uncompromising in form and argument. He
dissects the dehumanizing effects of colonialism,
arguing that it destroys the native sense of identity,
forcing people to adapt to an alien set of values—
including a core belief that they are inferior. This
results in deep psychological trauma.

Fanon's work played a pivotal role in the civil rights
movements of the 1960s.

Macat analyses are available from all good bookshops and libraries.

Access hundreds of analyses through one, multimedia tool.
Join free for one month **library.macat.com**

Macat Pairs

*Analyse historical and modern issues
from opposite sides of an argument.
Pairs include:*

INTERNATIONAL RELATIONS
IN THE 21ˢᵀ CENTURY

Samuel P. Huntington's
The Clash of Civilisations

In his highly influential 1996 book, Huntington offers a vision of a post-Cold War world in which conflict takes place not between competing ideologies but between cultures. The worst clash, he argues, will be between the Islamic world and the West: the West's arrogance and belief that its culture is a "gift" to the world will come into conflict with Islam's obstinacy and concern that its culture is under attack from a morally decadent "other."

Clash inspired much debate between different political schools of thought. But its greatest impact came in helping define American foreign policy in the wake of the 2001 terrorist attacks in New York and Washington.

Francis Fukuyama's
The End of History and the Last Man

Published in 1992, *The End of History and the Last Man* argues that capitalist democracy is the final destination for all societies. Fukuyama believed democracy triumphed during the Cold War because it lacks the "fundamental contradictions" inherent in communism and satisfies our yearning for freedom and equality. Democracy therefore marks the endpoint in the evolution of ideology, and so the "end of history." There will still be "events," but no fundamental change in ideology.

Macat analyses are available from all good bookshops and libraries.

Access hundreds of analyses through one, multimedia tool.
Join free for one month **library.macat.com**

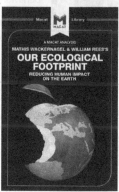

Macat Pairs

*Analyse historical and modern issues
from opposite sides of an argument.
Pairs include:*

Macat Pairs

*Analyse historical and modern issues from opposite sides of an argument.
Pairs include:*

HOW WE RELATE TO EACH OTHER AND SOCIETY

Jean-Jacques Rousseau's
The Social Contract

Rousseau's famous work sets out the radical concept of the 'social contract': a give-and-take relationship between individual freedom and social order.

If people are free to do as they like, governed only by their own sense of justice, they are also vulnerable to chaos and violence. To avoid this, Rousseau proposes, they should agree to give up some freedom to benefit from the protection of social and political organization. But this deal is only just if societies are led by the collective needs and desires of the people, and able to control the private interests of individuals. For Rousseau, the only legitimate form of government is rule by the people.

Robert D. Putnam's
Bowling Alone

In *Bowling Alone*, Robert Putnam argues that Americans have become disconnected from one another and from the institutions of their common life, and investigates the consequences of this change.

Looking at a range of indicators, from membership in formal organizations to the number of invitations being extended to informal dinner parties, Putnam demonstrates that Americans are interacting less and creating less "social capital" – with potentially disastrous implications for their society.

It would be difficult to overstate the impact of *Bowling Alone*, one of the most frequently cited social science publications of the last half-century.

Macat analyses are available from all good bookshops and libraries.

Access hundreds of analyses through one, multimedia tool.
Join free for one month **library.macat.com**